Praise for *Say More About That...*

"With this book, Amber Cabral delivers another timely gem. She is a gifted communicator, bringing concepts and techniques that are relatable and actionable. Now you can have her as a coach and advisor, too."
—Mark Breitbard, President and CEO, Global Gap Brand

"There is no one more qualified than Amber Cabral to teach on speaking up for yourself. I remember seeing Amber speaking at an inclusion summit for the first time. I was stunned. After working in corporate America for over a decade before starting my own company, I'd seen a lot, but her approach was refreshing, honest, and genuine. The room was mesmerized. Top executives were there taking notes! Presidents of Fortune 500 companies have shared the difference Amber has made in their lives and their business culture. This book, *Say More About That*, is a must-read."
—Brandice N. Daniel, CEO and Founder, Harlem's Fashion Row

"Amber Cabral's book *Say More About That. . .And Other Ways to Speak Up, Push Back, and Advocate for Yourself and Others* will do for you what meeting Amber and learning from her has done for me: help you understand the importance of having a voice and influencing change through inclusive and equitable behaviors. Her real-life examples and pragmatic approach to such a challenging topic will leave you with practical skills to be courageous and speak up on topics that matter."
—Brandy Sislow, Chief Human Resources Officer, Kendra Scott

"As a leading voice in the inclusion space, Amber continues to push the envelope to ensure that her books truly help people to realize their authentic selves. Her writing forces the reader to take a look not only *at* themselves but also deep *within* themselves. Amber never talks over you and instead speaks directly to you while also sharing her own journey to enlightenment. Speaking up is truly a skill that can be learned, and this book will help the reader to understand what that skill looks like so they can take meaningful action for themselves and others."
—Reginald J. Miller, VP, Global Chief Diversity, Equity, and Inclusion Officer, McDonald's

"*Say More About That* puts a spotlight on the importance of being part of the solution and using your position of privilege to advocate for those who do not have the same access. What makes Amber brilliant is her ability to simplify and effectively communicate complex issues. Her straightforward and practical advice on how you can foster a more equitable and inclusive culture has helped me gain useful perspectives I did not have before."

—Jyothi Rao, CEO, Intermix

"Continuing to share her wisdom and experience in this volume, Amber Cabral definitively proves that she is a consummate DEI professional. But rather than dispense theoretical thought leadership, Amber's strategic approach is delivered through impactful anecdotes and easy-to-follow instructions. Reading this, as well as her previous book, *Allies and Advocates*, is like having a good friend counsel you through challenging conversations both professionally and personally. Get copies for friends, family, and colleagues. They, and you, will be better for it."

—Lydia Dishman, Staff Editor, *Fast Company*

Say More About That...

Say More About That...

And Other Ways to
Speak Up,
Push Back,
and **Advocate**
for Yourself and Others

AMBER CABRAL

WILEY

Published by John Wiley & Sons, Inc., Hoboken, New Jersey.
Published simultaneously in Canada.

For general information on our other products and services or for technical support, please contact our Customer Care Department within the United States at (800) 762-2974, outside the United States at (317) 572-3993 or fax (317) 572-4002.

Wiley also publishes its books in a variety of electronic formats. Some content that appears in print may not be available in electronic formats. For more information about Wiley products, visit our web site at www.wiley.com.

Library of Congress Cataloging-in-Publication Data:

Names: Cabral, Amber, author.
Title: Say more about that. . . : and other ways to speak up, push
   back, and advocate for yourself and others / Amber Cabral.
Description: Hoboken, New Jersey : Wiley, [2022] | Includes index.
Identifiers: LCCN 2022012515 (print) | LCCN 2022012516 (ebook) | ISBN
   9781119839323 (cloth) | ISBN 9781119839347 (adobe pdf) | ISBN 9781119839330 (epub)
Subjects: LCSH: Self-reliance. | Courage.
Classification: LCC BJ1533.S27 C33 2022 (print) | LCC BJ1533.S27 (ebook)
   | DDC 158.1—dc23/eng/20220407

LC record available at https://lccn.loc.gov/2022012515
LC ebook record available at https://lccn.loc.gov/2022012516

Cover Background Texture: © GETTY IMAGES | MFTO
Cover Design: Paul McCarthy

SKY10033883_060222

For Pammy

You get a choice: How do you want your life to feel?

Content Warning

This book covers subject matter and uses examples for learning purposes that some folks may find discriminatory, frustrating, uncomfortable, or microaggressive. I have tried to be as responsible and thoughtful as possible in covering identity-related content in this book because I want this to be a useful resource to help people to communicate. Also, given the speed at which the inclusion and equity space changes and the speed that information moves at these days, it is possible that some content or framing in this book may fall into or out of favor by the time you read it. I am subject to error, bias, and plain old poor judgment, so although I tried my very best to be responsible, respectful, and compassionate in my delivery, there may be some places in this book where I missed the mark. My hope is that you are able to find value, resource, and relief in these pages and are also able to grant grace to me in the spaces where I fall short on anticipating your needs as a reader.

Contents

Foreword by Amanda Miller Littlejohn xv

Acknowledgments xxi

Introduction xxiii

PART I Getting Grounded in the Fundamentals 1

1 Identity 3

2 Inclusion 7

3 Bias 15

4 Feedback 19

5 Privilege 25

6 Allyship and Advocacy 31

7 Equity 33

PART II Understanding the Landscape 37

8 Overcoming the Most Common Obstacles 39

9 Why Is Pushing Back So Hard? 57

10 Critical Communication Tools 65

11 Performative Allyship and Advocacy 81

12 Pushing Back and Speaking Up – A Pep Talk 91

PART III Language and Tactics 99

13 A Short Lesson on Boundaries and Staying
    Focused on the Goal 101

14 Avoid People-Pleasing and Resentment 107

15 Dealing with Professional Gaslighting. 111

16 Saying No While Still Protecting Your Reputation 113

17 Intimidation: But What If They Know More Than
I Do? 119

18 Power Imbalance: What If I Am Not the One with the
Power? 123

19 Microaggressions: What If I Am Encountering a
Microaggression? 127

20 Disrespected: What If Someone Is Blatantly
Mistreating Me or Crossing a Line? 135

21 Underrepresented: What If I Am the Only One? 139

22 Dismissed: What If I Am Not Feeling Heard? 143

23 Medical Advocacy: When Feeling Intimidated,
Dismissed, and Powerless Combine 147

24 Interrupted: What If I Keep Getting Talked Over? 155

25 Framework: How to Speak Up and Advocate for
Yourself and Others 161

26 It's a Conversation, Not a Confrontation. 169

27 Keeping the Temperature Down in Tough Discussions .175

28 Any Questions? 183

29 Be Good to Yourself 191

About the Author 193

Index. 195

Foreword

When I started my business in the late aughts, I quickly realized how critical speaking up to defend myself and enforce my boundaries would be to my ultimate success. Whether I needed to speak up to negotiate for more money or enforce contract terms to avoid scope creep, I learned early on how challenged I was without that natural ability. I'm not proud to admit that I passed up clients, projects, and key business relationships all because I lacked the tools to advocate for myself and my needs. It was easier to just let some opportunities go, even if I didn't want to. But how did I get so woefully skilled at staying silent?

Upon reflection, I can see how the societal, cultural, and family contexts in which I was raised all played a part. I came of age in the eighties and nineties, in an America where women were expected to acquiesce; where daring to ask questions or voice an unpopular opinion undermined your likability. But I also grew up Black, where dissent could get you labeled angry or difficult and undermine your prospects for upward mobility. And beyond all that, I grew up in a Black southern Christian home where girls like me were expected to defer to their elders at all costs. If you chose to question an adult's authority in the family or church you were labeled "disrespectful," and in some cases that label undermined your physical safety.

Against this backdrop, I was an unusually smart and intellectually curious Black girl growing up in the South. I constantly had questions that needed answers, but being repeatedly shut down when my innocent need to know made others feel tired or inconvenienced certainly discouraged my desire to speak up.

I learned early on that sometimes my mind moved faster than my mouth should; that, in consideration of others, I should stifle the urge to voice the questions, concerns, or protests that came so naturally to me. It's a learning you get in different ways and from different people, but a lesson that, whether explicitly stated or subtly implied, ultimately comes through crystal clear: *shut up.*

I heard, intimated, or physically felt that phrase so early and often in my life, I can't even remember the point when I let it seep deep inside, redefining my style of response. But I distinctly remember the feeling of being small, brown, and powerless. Even more, I distinctly remember how meaningless it felt to have things to say or share because no one with power cared enough to hear me out. Or worse, because of their power, if they didn't want to hear what I had to say they could silence me with an icy stare.

So at some point along the way, I muted my own voice. At those pivotal life stages when you're supposed to be building the muscle to speak up for yourself or advocate for others, I unknowingly let mine grow weak from disuse. And I'm not the only one. When faced with a situation that required a quick comeback, or the words to set someone straight, I'd freeze. My mind would race, trying to identify my argument as well as the words to make it, but never in enough time to seize the moment and salvage the situation. I'd feel a range of emotions depending on the situation and size of the audience who may have witnessed my silence – from irritated and angry to humiliated and embarrassed that I'd let the moment pass without saying what needed to be said.

After steadily building a business helping high-achieving professionals create visibility around their gifts, I learned I wasn't alone in my loss for words. When witnessing legions of talented, accomplished professionals – the majority of them Black women – struggle to speak up and put themselves out there, I saw the other side of the visibility coin. Because they'd been socialized like me to *be good girls and stay quiet*, many of my clients found that the act of making noise about who they were and what they had to offer required practice. Like mine, their muscles for speaking up – in this case about themselves and their skills – had never been given the chance to develop.

It was truly a revelation then to meet Amber Cabral at a conference in 2015. After connecting briefly, she became a client; we went on to work together, and eventually became good friends. But from the moment we connected, I saw a rare and unique quality absent in me and many of the women I coach. Amber was not at all afraid to speak up. This woman was not one to be messed with! Instead of shrinking back from an uncomfortable conversation, Amber would puff up and speak up. Instead of simply going along to keep the peace or spare someone else's feelings, Amber was willing to disrupt the status quo if that meant rightness and justice would prevail.

At the heart of this I came to understand was her authenticity – she had that rare inability to be duplicitous. If she disagreed, felt something was unfair, or noticed someone being taken advantage of, she wouldn't let it slide. She was always ready to call out bad behavior and hold people accountable for their actions, no matter what. And Amber never seemed to worry if people wouldn't like her; she would speak up anyway. Ironically, I think she won more friends because of that.

Also at the heart of this willingness was her passion for fairness. It's no surprise she's built a wildly successful business teaching organizations how to make things more equitable, more fair for everyone. This passion and appetite for fairness drives her business, but, at a more essential level, drives that part of her that will speak up for you even when you can't.

At first, I thought Amber was "lucky" to somehow always instinctively know when and how to speak up productively. But the more I hung around her, the more I realized it's a skill that anyone can develop with practice.

As a coach, I've had the honor of witnessing her gifts and teaching her some new skills. But as is the case with my best clients, I've had the opportunity to learn more from her than I could have ever imagined. Beyond her clear gift for diversity equity and inclusion strategy, Amber is truly a genius at crafting the credible comeback that will reposition you, take back your power, and shift the dynamic of an encounter. She has a gift for giving you language to be brave when you know you should say something but aren't quite sure what that something is. The process isn't always pretty, but it's a skill you should always be able to access when you need it.

I've witnessed, supported, and worked with hundreds of high achievers along my journey and never have I met someone so in command of their ability to advocate for themselves and others. I have been Amber's coach turned friend, and she has personally given me language to maintain my boundaries or hold others accountable for their bad behavior. And sometimes, she's just plain spoken up on my behalf, which is what any good advocate does.

On more than one occasion she's given me language to speak up for myself. Whether it was telling me what to say to a doctor who was dismissing my concerns about my son's asthma medication, or helping me craft a response to a lowball offer from a new corporate client, she's repeatedly given me the words to say to help me feel seen and heard. I count on her to give me scripts to ensure an equitable outcome when I'm not the one in the position of power. I'm thrilled she was generous enough to write this book so she could share them with you, too.

When George Floyd was murdered at the hands of Minneapolis police officers, a community of bystanders looked on. Even fellow officers who had more institutional power to intervene and save a life did not. I sometimes wonder whether Derek Chauvin's fellow officers thought to speak up at any point during the over eight minutes Chauvin's knee pressed the life out of Floyd's dying body. Would they have intervened if they had known what to do? Would they have said something if only they'd known what to say to diffuse the situation?

Just a few weeks prior to me writing these words, a young woman boarded a subway train and was assaulted in front of her fellow passengers. When the perpetrator sat down beside her and groped at her sexually despite her protests for 40 minutes, no one spoke up and came to her aid. Instead the other passengers filmed the incident.

Why?

These days, it seems that instead of speaking up to stop unlawful or unfair acts from occurring, our collective reflex is to grab our smartphones and film what we see. Whether this video evidence is leading to more justice is debatable, but one thing is certain: wrongdoers are emboldened by silence. When we see something and don't say something, we are in some ways complicit; our silence gives bad behavior the oxygen it needs to persist.

I fear this new tendency to record instead of speak up sets a dangerous precedent for women, people of color, members of the LGBTQIA+ community, people with disabilities, and neurodivergent folks who have always been more vulnerable to harassment and physical attack. I fear for my infant daughter growing up in a world in which you could be raped on a subway train while a dozen other people watch on. I fear for my teen sons who could be killed at the hands of a police officer whose colleagues won't speak up and intervene to prevent a murder.

But my fear is tempered with hope, as I assume yours is or else you wouldn't be holding this book. Where so many of us shrink in fear or freeze and lose access to our words, Amber has hers within reach and is willing to bravely use them at all times. And an even greater gift is that she's willing to share a bit of her magic and show us how to do the same.

Amber and the events of our society have shown me that the muscle to speak up is not an optional one to cultivate – it's critical. When we find ourselves facing off against those who make it a common practice to abuse their power, "I didn't know what to say . . ." is no longer a reasonable excuse. We must intentionally build the muscle to speak up; sometimes life is literally on the line.

In some ways, I selfishly encouraged Amber to write this book because it was the manual I always needed. In many ways, this book is for me.

But I know I am not the only one who struggles with knowing what to say in heated situations, and even the tricky exchanges of everyday life. And I know how much having the right words at your disposal can give you the confidence to push back and speak up – even when it may be more comfortable to stay silent.

To those who were taught not to "meddle" but often feel called to use their privilege for the sake of someone else, this book is for you.

To those who are tired of feeling ill-equipped to negotiate, set a boundary, call out bad behavior, or stand up to people in positions of power, this book is for you.

To those who were silenced so much early on that self-silencing also became the norm, this book is for you, too. This book is for us. It's not too late to unmute ourselves. Using the tools in this book, we can build a new muscle. We can reclaim our power to speak up for ourselves, for others, for when it matters the most.

For all the times we've seen something, said nothing, and regretted staying silent, we finally have the words.

Amanda Miller Littlejohn
Writer, executive branding coach, and
founder of Package Your Genius Academy

Acknowledgments

Sincere appreciation to all the folks who sent food, checked in, polled folks for titles, or otherwise nudged me to get this book done. I needed it. Your support and the enormous value you place on my teeny, little contributions to this world are not unnoticed. I'm more grateful for you than I could ever effectively articulate.

Special thanks to:

My sister (and the best human ever), Rin Price

Amanda Miller Littlejohn

Jeanenne Ray

Adaobi Obi Tulton

Lauren Ware

Kirstie Gardner

Aimee L. Strang

Jonathan M. Kester, Esq.

Mark and Halle Millien

Jonathon and Kisha Modica

Mike Thompson and Lynn Wong

Mercedes Posey

Joshua Spivey

James E. Estes

Introduction

What a time to be alive. No matter when you are reading this book, likely you are experiencing some kind of changes and shifts such that a book about pushing back is even on your radar. I am so glad you are here! We all need the skill to push back and appropriately challenge. It is indeed essential to getting what we need and want in our lives. Doing it isn't easy, though, and since it is something I work with clients on regularly, I thought it might be useful to collect some of the most common ideas and tactics in one place for anyone to reference.

I am writing this in 2021, following the unforgettable year, 2020, when dual pandemics swept the globe: the COVID-19 viral pandemic and a race, identity, and social justice pandemic after the widely publicized murder of George Floyd. These two major events called everything into question, from how we work, to how we communicate, to how we understand identity. Conversations about identity, race, and politics became more commonplace, but also more complex. In an attempt to provide some guidance and support for what would turn out to be the start of a massive culture shift, I wrote my first book, titled *Allies and Advocates: Creating an Inclusive and Equitable Culture*, which released at the end of 2020. Allyship and advocacy were suddenly topics everyone wanted to understand as folks came to grips with the fallout after the murder of George Floyd and the desire to show up for marginalized and oppressed people came with questions like "How do I serve as an ally?" I wrote *Allies and Advocates* as an answer to that question. The book takes an exploratory walk through terminology common to the inclusion and equity space and through definitions, activities, and real-world examples, helps folks understand what steps are necessary to be an ally and an advocate. It's a great place to start if you are new to the inclusion and equity space.

In the time since the release of *Allies and Advocates*, I have started to notice some new trends in the inclusion and equity space. Most notably, while some have felt more empowered to speak up and try to serve as allies and advocates for themselves, their communities, and people experiencing oppression, others have slunk to the false safety of silence, snarky comments, and data consumption without taking any real-world action. The latter isn't just unhelpful, it's problematic.

Inclusion and equity work is an ongoing series of behavior and mindset shifts that move our culture forward over time. Either you are on board or you are an obstacle. If you are on board you should expect to be in a perpetual state of learning, growing, taking feedback, and evolving your perspectives and behaviors as to what inclusion and equity mean in modern times. Being on board means recognizing there is not a destination, there is not a good enough, there is always, always a way to be better – a better ally, a more inclusive leader, an advocate for someone, a learner, a teacher, a partner in ensuring equitable experiences are accessible for an all that is always evolving.

If we want inclusion to stop being a hypothetical and mythical place to aspire to, we have to be willing to activate it in the real world. In this follow-up to *Allies and Advocates*, I hope to help you see how your learnings apply to real-life, day-to-day interactions. This book is full of examples that have been plucked from reality. Where *Allies and Advocates* was an introductory and instructional guidebook aiming to transfer foundational knowledge and to define the basics of allyship, advocacy and being inclusive, *Say More About That . . . And Other Ways to Speak Up, Push Back, and Advocate for Yourself and Others* is the practicum, where you learn by doing. This book will have plenty of questions to consider and tactics to employ, but the approach in this book is geared more toward working your muscles around inclusion, rather than affirming the core knowledge essential to being an ally and an advocate. Speaking up is a muscle.

My Story – How'd I Get So Good at Speaking Up?

Usually after someone witnesses me pushing back about something, they ask me how I got so good at doing it. It is funny because I don't even think much about it; I just do it. Who we are truly is a combination of our life experiences, and honestly, with my upbringing, a lot of times I had to speak up or go without. I also always was concerned about fairness, even as a child. I wanted the same things everyone else had. I didn't like when I got less of anything because I was a girl or younger or smaller or whatever arbitrary measure folks used, so I learned early to challenge and question.

The first time I remember deliberately challenging something was when I was in grade school. I always struggled with the letter "z" because it was the only letter that didn't have an ascender or descender (like letters "b" or "j") that opened facing the opposite direction of the other letters. Letters "e," "r," and, probably most notably, "s" all opened facing the same direction. It made no sense that "z" went the other way. Even when I would be reading and come across a z, it looked backward to me. So, at some point, before first grade, I started writing them the opposite way; the way they looked correct to me. I was a pretty good student and had good grades, and teachers would just circle my z's to show me they were wrong. I hardly ever lost points for it – until about halfway through second grade. My teacher literally told me one day, "This homework deserves an A, and I am going to give you an A this time, but the next time I see a backwards z in your work, the whole paper will fail." I tried explaining my logic, but the teacher didn't want to hear it. My teacher shared with me that she meant what she'd said and sent me home with a note for me to give to my mother expressing what she'd told me about my z's.

My mother sat me down and asked me, "Why do you write your z's backwards?" She said, "Many teachers have mentioned it and they were not concerned because they expected that you would have corrected it by now. This teacher thinks you are doing it on purpose."

"I am doing it on purpose," I explained. Then, I told her why. I remember her listening and then smiling and saying, "That makes sense. In life, though, the thing that makes sense to us isn't always how it's going to work out. It is okay to try, but sometimes we should pick our battles. Maybe since everyone in the world does it this way and already understands it, it is okay for you to let this battle go." Needless to say, I did, and my z's are written correctly – though, secretly, I still question why the letter goes that way.

My upbringing was not without flaws; I grew up in a single-parent home and there was a litany of obstacles between then and now that I have encountered to make it to where I am today. Just like many of you, I have my wounds from the journey, because, after all, no one makes it to adulthood without scars. Growing up, I do remember my mother usually being willing to listen to my logic and ideas, though. I remember her challenging teachers when I told her I didn't think I was being treated fairly. I also remember her encouraging me to ask questions of folks with authority, like at visits to the doctor or dentist. I accompanied her to parent–teacher conferences, where I recall most parents attended without their kids. If I had to guess, I imagine my willingness to speak up started with my mother always encouraging me to speak up in situations like these, starting when I was under the age of 10.

As I got older, I continued to stand up for myself on all kinds of things. From pushing back on college professors' grading scales to calling the cell phone company about errors on my bill, I learned early that if you don't say anything, it can cost you. When you are younger it costs you grades and a few extra bucks on a small bill, but the costs add up as you age to include bigger and more costly losses. Not speaking up can cost you the respect of those around you, it can cost you the equity of being paid fairly, and it can even cost you access to opportunity – all because you didn't say anything. I don't know about you, but I want all the options, the choices, the vastness of chance, so I am going to ask for them! And when the answer is no, I am going to ask why. I am going to always press for equity and will not hesitate to adjust how I spend my time, presence, or dollars in lieu of contributing to injustice in any way. There have been some losses because I pushed back – some jobs, some friends, some opportunities – but nothing that was worth holding on to when I look back and truly consider how I was being treated.

I will be candid: I had to learn *how* to push back. In my younger years, I'd get frustrated and loud and snappy when I identified an injustice. My quick-witted snarky responses impacted me in some tough ways; I struggled to get promoted in companies and at one point was suspended for how I spoke to a leader. A couple of romantic relationships ended because of how I talked to my boyfriend. I had to learn how to speak up, and it took some years, but now I know just how to appropriately push back without doing the kind of damage that can hold me back. I understand now that there is a way to say anything and have it land well, even if it stings a little.

I also understand that when I don't speak up and I let things slide, it doesn't impact just me – it impacts many other things I may not immediately see, because we are all a part of the system. The turbulence of recent years has a lot of folks talking about the systems we operate in and the bias that shows up in them. From human resources, to technology, to the government – folks are becoming better able to understand how systems and the processes within those systems can oppress different types of people. Although in some cases you hear about calls to address the many biases and the discrimination folks are uncovering, other times folks say nothing, and whatever the systemic problems are, they just continue. The longer a problem goes on, the more folks it can impact and, for me, that usually makes me want to speak up.

Speaking up about every single thing is unreasonable – we'd never be able to move forward in life that way. So, I try to speak up in three main circumstances in my own life. They are as follows:

1. When I am not being treated fairly. I have to protect myself, so I always speak up when I am not being included or am experiencing inequity.
2. When I notice someone else isn't being treated fairly and I have the ability to speak up. When I say ability, I mean that I am able to say something and I am not risking being physically or emotionally harmed or attacked. This one is tricky because in 2021, folks like to pretend that hurt feelings are actual harm. The fact is, feelings are going to get hurt just living everyday life!
3. When I have the power or influence to change whatever is going on. I am always open to making adjustments to include folks or be more equitable with anything I control or have a say over.

It is possible that you did not have a parent who gave you the permission as a child to ask questions, challenge the status quo, or query authority figures. If you didn't build the muscle young, it is not too late. You still can start to push back, and the three areas above might be good starting points to give you an idea of where and when you should speak up. As you read, you will learn skills and tactics to help you know what and how to say things when the opportunity to speak up arises – even if you have to do it scared.

Speaking of scared, speaking up takes consistent practice and bravery. Although most of my friends consider speaking up to be a core part of my identity, I still get nervous about doing it. I get that weird feeling in my belly or my chest, too. At times, I too have to take a moment to figure out the right approach and the right words for each moment. I get better and better the more I push through and do it, though. The same is true for you; the more you speak up and advocate for yourself and others, the easier it becomes to spot when something isn't right and to actually build up the nerve to say something to address it.

Allies and Advocates Must Master Taking Action

In *Allies and Advocates,* I cover speaking up as one of the actions that are critical for anyone to consider themselves an ally or an advocate. Specifically, I remind folks that speaking up is a brave thing. When you decide it is important to action on inclusion and equity, you will discover a number of opportunities to speak up, and a number of them will feel challenging. Think about how many times you have suffered bad service in a restaurant and simply said to yourself, "I just won't be back." A good amount of the time we will not speak up for ourselves, let alone speak up for others. We aren't brave enough to get past the idea that it is going to be a challenging discussion, so we will settle for unfair treatment, often out of fear of confrontation. What we fail to consider when we make these compromises is that the person who treats us poorly will continue, often oblivious, to mistreat other people. There is nothing inclusive or equitable about that.

It doesn't matter how many programs, speakers, and toolkits you build or buy. Inclusion and equity cannot be purchased or manufactured by outside consultants. Each individual person who is a part of a culture or community must act on inclusion and equity for them to happen. Whether in the workplace or in the nation, the path to inclusion and equity requires that you change how you behave, and everyone else around you has to be willing to do the same. Learning inclusive and equitable behaviors is not something you pick up in a book or training. It is something you learn by participating in a culture where you give feedback (which requires you to speak up) and you receive feedback (which requires those around you to speak up). You can't move toward inclusive and equitable treatment without people speaking up. You won't know if you are mispronouncing someone's name if they do not speak up. No one knows if they are gendering you incorrectly if you do not speak up. I won't know that a behavior was culturally inappropriate if no one tells me. The failure to push back, speak up, and challenge ideas leads to costly reputation damage every single day. Consider these few incidents over the past few years:

■ In 2019, luxury fashion house Gucci received backlash for its turtleneck jumper with a balaclava cutout around the mouth, lined with oversized red lips that resembled blackface. Gucci removed the $890 item from its online and physical locations and issued an apology. Blackface, a type of performance where a white person applies black makeup to mock Black people, has a long and troublesome history in the United States especially, but has also been performed in other parts of the world as well. What might have happened instead if someone had spoken up at the product shoot about the design, or perhaps even someone on the design team had spoken up earlier?

- Snickers launched an ad in Spain in which a Spanish influencer flamboyantly orders a drink, obviously flirting with the waiter. They then take a bite of a Snickers ice cream bar and turn into a traditionally masculine man. The ad was pulled after being criticized as homophobic. What might have happened if someone had spoken up during the review of the commercial's script?

- Facebook users watched a video featuring Black men in altercations with white civilians and police officers. Users who watched the video saw an automated prompt from the social network that asked if they would like to "keep seeing videos about primates," although the video had no primates in it. Facebook claims its artificial intelligence (AI) software incorrectly categorized the video, but consider for a moment where AI learns how and what to categorize. What might have happened if someone of influence had raised some concerns about how technology wasn't inclusive with the AI product?

Speaking up is often where inclusion starts, and it is always going to be how it moves forward. I know speaking up can be risky. In any of the situations just presented, someone could be afraid to speak up because they are afraid of losing their job. Concerns about losing one's job or otherwise being in some sort of danger are valid, and if that is your circumstance, you probably do not feel confident about your ability to speak up. If you are at a company that is not committed to actually being inclusive or shifting their culture, then your ability to push back is absent. There are no tactics to manage that. I encourage everyone to consider their personal circumstances and needs alongside the recommendations and techniques in this book. You should always prioritize your safety and well-being.

That said, inclusion and equity cannot happen without speaking up. That's likely a tough pill to swallow for some folks, but it is true. Every time I teach speaking up in the courses I facilitate, folks express all kinds of concerns around it. I hear concerns like, "How do I speak up with my leader?" and "What if I am the only woman in the room?" Sometimes the concern is that folks don't know what to say or are afraid to be the only one doing the challenging. The consistent questions around how to speak up and what to say is exactly why I decided to tackle this topic as the follow-up to *Allies and Advocates*. There are ways to speak up for yourself and for others that don't have to mean you are ruining your reputation or career. There are also obstacles that I hear, over and over, to folks speaking up that you can manage and appropriately challenge, so let's discuss some of those.

What Gets in the Way: Obstacles to Speaking Up

In the work I do, I hear a lot of people saying they want their workplaces, kids' schools, and communities to be more inclusive, but when inclusion isn't happening, people are not saying anything about it. When someone does something patently exclusive or even offensive, no one is holding anyone accountable. Everyone is just sitting by while all kinds of inequitable behaviors unfold. Folks are allowing people to talk over others in meetings. Folks are laughing off or ignoring racist microaggressions. People are opting to ignore when people are repeatedly using the wrong pronouns. In fact, sometimes it seems like folks are more apt to pull their phones out and record an incident, or talk to their friends and colleagues about something that happened, than to speak up in the moment. By no means am I suggesting that anyone should put themselves in harm's way, but far too often folks are sitting by silently when inappropriate and noninclusive behaviors are happening that could be interrupted if someone simply spoke up. I am often asked questions like "what should I say?" or "how do I handle it when … ?" about inequitable or noninclusive behaviors, and often it comes down to a few things that cause people to get hung up and to stay silent:

- Understanding: This might sound like "I don't know if I understand/agree/believe that disabled people face discrimination, so I am just going to be quiet."

- Accountability: This might sound like "I don't think my leader understands/agrees/believes in inclusion, so I don't know how to hold them accountable for not being inclusive."
- Fear: This might sound like "I am afraid to say something in case it is the wrong thing to say."
- Discomfort: This might sound like "I am uncomfortable talking about racial equity." Or it can sound like "I am afraid of making others uncomfortable by addressing inequitable behaviors."
- Time: This might sound like "I don't have the time to correct every single person I encounter." Or it can sound like "We are moving so quickly, I don't have the time to be inclusive."

I get it. Each of these can feel like a lot to take on. Plus, when you consider our busy personal lives and the totally bizarre times folks all around the globe are experiencing since the pandemic changed our lives in 2020, inclusion and equity can sometimes seem like a tad too much to take on. Believe it or not, though, all of these obstacles keeping us silent are things that we can get out of the way of us being inclusive, and while it will take some work, it isn't the kind of labor you think. In fact, in Part II of this book, we are going to talk about how to overcome the five obstacles I listed in this section, all with tactics that you can put into action right away.

How This Book Is Structured

I recognize that in the work of inclusion we all can wear a myriad of hats. Sometimes we are marginalized, sometimes we are allies or advocates, and sometimes with the richness in our identities we can be a little of each. I worked to frame everything from as many perspectives as I could. So as you read and find in some places that you are on the side of privilege and power and operating as an ally or an advocate, there are techniques and resources for you. If you find in other places that you are marginalized, there are techniques and resources for you, too. Inclusion and equity belong to all of us, so I tried to make this book one that anyone can pick up and find resources within.

This book is split into three parts. Part I: Getting Grounded in the Fundamentals is focused on introducing or reintroducing some of the foundational language and concepts of inclusion. While speaking up and pushing back are not always connected to inclusion, usually they are connected to some perceived inequity. Understanding foundational concepts and language around inclusion and equity is helpful. Additionally, I work to go a step beyond core definitions and get into some of the nuance in each concept. We will cover inclusion, equity, bias, privilege, and a few others that you have probably heard of but perhaps have not considered in the depth that they will be explored in this book.

Part II: Understanding the Landscape is focused on understanding the landscape that we are navigating when it comes to speaking up. Here we will dig into some of the common concerns about speaking up, like the kinds of obstacles you might encounter and how your personal culture and American culture can make speaking up hard, and explore critical communication tools and mindsets that can help you push past the obstacles that commonly arise. This section of the book will help make the last part of the book actionable.

Part III: Language and Tactics is about giving you the words and the techniques to use when you need to speak up. In this section of the book you will find scripts you can use for some common circumstances where speaking up or pushing back is important for you to thrive, be inclusive, and bring equity to life. You will also find techniques to help you pivot when speaking up enflames a situation and how to exit a conversation with grace.

Candidly, this book won't cover every scenario. My hope is that I have put together a resource that will help you fortify your role as an ally, an advocate, and a champion of inclusion and equity with language that helps you confidently challenge and shift perspectives in the workplace, at home, and in your day-to-day life. I hope you find strength and confidence where they are thin, and that you also grow to see disagreements or differences in perspectives as opportunities you can manage instead of circumstances to shrink under.

Let's get started.

Getting Grounded in the Fundamentals

In my first book, *Allies and Advocates*, I define a lot of the key terms that are helpful in navigating inclusive and equitable discussions. In this book, the goal is to help you better position yourself with inclusion and equity so you can start truly considering what it means to embed an inclusive mindset into your day-to-day life. Knowing the language of diversity, equity, and inclusion is one thing; actually taking action in a meaningful way is significantly more impactful. So in this first part of the book, let's get intimately acquainted (or in some cases, reacquainted) with some of the common terminology and concepts common to the inclusion and equity space. By intimately acquainted I mean moving beyond core definitions accompanied by a few examples. Instead, I want to help you see how these foundational principles can help you create more inclusive and equitable spaces, and understand some of the nuance that gets overlooked in the noise. In this part of the book, I hope to counter misinformation and perspectives that can be obstructive to moving inclusion and equity forward. Most importantly, through real-life examples and stories, I want to arm you with a personal connection to bringing inclusion to life.

Let's dig into some terms and concepts.

1 Identity

Identity is the myriad of attributes and characteristics that make us who we are. Elements like gender, age, race, sexual orientation, religion, income, height, personal style, and even languages spoken are all aspects of identity. There are so many elements that can fall under identity – in addition to those just mentioned, it includes physical appearance, parental status, political affiliation, ethnicity, and much more. Identity is what all the fuss is about. We do great at embracing identities that we have seen before or are familiar with, but really have a difficult time when there's someone with an identity we don't understand or haven't seen before. Some of us start referencing whatever stereotypes we have heard or we keep our distance and even stare.

A few things are really important to know about identity that can help you navigate interactions with identities you have never encountered before responsibly:

1. Identity is a shared experience in that we identify people all the time without even thinking about it: tall, small, thin, male, rich, smart, married – but just because you have identified a person doesn't mean that is how they identify themselves. Just as your identity is yours alone and you know it intimately, other folks are the same with theirs.

2. Identity, while it is shared, it is also incredibly personal. There are aspects of your identity that maybe only you know about. Not all aspects of identity are visible, and of those that are, not all of the assumptions we make about what we see are accurate. We assume what another's gender, income status, race, ethnicity, and more are based on appearance, presence, personal style – all kinds of things. Those assumptions are not always correct. When it comes to identity, be open to correction when you are wrong.

3. Folks are more than just one story. The White girl with the fun hair is more than her unique look, the tall Black man is more than his height, the woman with the Spanish accent is more than her speech, you are more than whatever folks tend to readily identify about you. People are more than just one story, and collectively, we can all do better at making room to learn those stories instead of assuming people are one thing, or that the thing we see is the most important thing about their identity to them. Remind yourself when encountering folks that they are more than what you have decided about them in the first few minutes, just as you are.

4. No one knows you better than you. The same is true for others. This is why it is imperative that you call folks what they want to be called. This goes for names, pronouns, nicknames, and titles. If someone refers to themselves as Nathaniel, don't call them Nate. If someone tells you their pronouns are they/them, use those pronouns. I get that you might not understand or want to probe – and perhaps as you build more relationships with a variety of people, you might learn folks' personal whys. Even in the absence of understanding, you can still be respectful.

Identity is super complex and it is evolving. We have identities that we hang on to for our whole lives; in my case, my name will always be Amber Cabral. We also have identities that we only have for a short time, like, in my case, college student or ballerina. Society and the way our brains work around bias (which I cover later in this part of the book) have gotten most of us in the habit of casually identifying people and getting defensive when we are wrong. Practice letting go of the idea that you know anything about anyone's identity besides your own.

A Note about Identity and Pronouns

Pronoun use is one that people ask me about often, so I want to lean in a little more on this aspect of identity. Usually I am asked something like, "How do I get in the habit of using 'they' in the singular when it isn't proper English and it wasn't what I was taught?" First, likely you've used they in the singular before when you didn't know who someone was. For example, you learn that there will be a new CEO of your company soon, but you don't know who it will be. You might say something like "I don't know who they will be, but I am looking forward to learning their new leadership style." There it is, they in the singular. Another example: you find a set of keys in the shopping mall one day; you might give them to the lost and found and say, "I don't who these keys belong to, but they left them in the toy store." There it is: they in the singular, again.

Second, there are a great many things you have been taught that you have had to unlearn. I hear many new parents talk about how they want to parent differently than they were parented. You can expand your skillset beyond what you were taught when you are exposed to new things. That exposure to new things might be meeting other parents through parenting groups, talking with your parent friends, or even joining the parents' resource group at your job if they have one. This willingness to learn so you can change your behavior (whether parenting is your thing or it is something else) is called having a growth mindset. A growth mindset means you believe that your basic characteristics can be cultivated through application and experience. It is the idea that you can evolve, learn, and improve as you learn more. A growth mindset is the ideal lens to approach inclusion and equity because it encourages the openness necessary to invite growth – like being receptive to folks using different pronouns. Having a growth mindset also helps us all to engage in conversations around identity, life experiences, and interpersonal differences respectfully, because it pushes judgment aside in favor of learning.

Third, you can practice pronouns. For the next week, use gender-neutral language in all of your conversations. When you slip up and default to the binary he or she, correct yourself in the moment. Do it with everyone. The thing about gender-neutral language is that most folks are not offended by it, so folks are unlikely to correct you – but if they do, then remember number 4 above: call folks what they want to be called. If someone happens to ask you why you are using they/them pronouns, you can let them know you are practicing; you never know, you might gain an accountability partner from the conversation.

Another way you can practice if you are in an organization that encourages putting pronouns in signatures, on nametags, or in Zoom titles is to actually read folks' pronoun placements and use them. Many times these placements just act as additional labels that people ignore. I don't love the practice of using pronouns in signatures, on nametags, or in Zoom titles because I don't often see it implemented well. Meaning, everyone might be invited or encouraged to share their pronouns, but there isn't much supplemental action or accountability around it – like educating folks on how to correct someone when they are misgendered, or setting the expectation that you may be corrected on pronouns. So it feels performative. But when there are labels provided, you can, as a matter of personal practice, actively pay attention to them. In Part III of this book I make some recommendations on how to speak up when you are misidentified or speak up for others who have the experience of being misidentified.

Pronouns are just one part of identity, so remember to be open to other adjustments around other aspects of identity as well. Some folks won't want to be sir or ma'am even if the terms align with their gender. Some folks are sensitive about nicknames or abbreviations of their name. Just stay flexible, and if you are not sure, you can always ask, "I just want to check in, am I calling you how you want to be called?" If they say no, ask for clarity and invite them to correct you when you get it wrong. That invitation might sound like "I know it isn't easy to correct when folks make this mistake, but if you are willing, I would welcome you correcting me."

These things are not hard; they are new. They are also very simple adjustments, but they are not easy because we have habits already. Try not to see adjusting to correctly identify folks as "hard" or "challenging," and certainly don't tell folks you think respecting their identity is hard. How would you feel if someone regularly butchered your name and then said, "Your name is just so hard"? It's your name! We can all flex; we just need a bit of practice.

2 Inclusion

Inclusion has been a buzzword for a decade or more, but despite the popularity of the term, there is still quite a bit of confusion that exists around inclusion. If we are going to be able to effectively challenge and push back so we can advocate for ourselves and for others, then having a good working knowledge of what inclusion means and how it shows up in our lives is super critical.

I define inclusion as valuing, supporting, and connecting with people with unique beliefs, experiences, identities, ideas, opinions, and styles. It requires intentional behaviors, mindfulness, respect, and consideration of others. The work of including others, by definition, is one of the very few things on this earth that belongs to everyone; it must for everyone to have a sense of belonging. We are trying to bring everyone along on the journey to being valued, supported, and connected. We are trying to make sure as many people as possible get to have a sense of belonging in their workplaces, play spaces, and home spaces. I remind my clients all the time that inclusion doesn't belong to me – if inclusion is only palpable when I am working with your organization, then we are missing some important actions. So let's walk through some of the places folks can get stuck activating it in their lives.

When in conversations I ask why people hesitate to take action on inclusion, one of the most common responses I have heard is "I am not a leader in the diversity space." Guess what – that is just fine. The work of inclusion doesn't rest on just leaders; it requires all of us, so don't worry as much about being a "diversity leader." Instead, focus on leading inclusively, which is a matter of principles and actions, just like being a supportive leader or an innovative one. Do you strive to be an inclusive communicator? Do you work to ensure that your team, family, or friends get to have a sense of belonging in your space? Are you able to meaningfully apologize? (I cover how to meaningfully apologize in Chapter 4, Feedback). Are you willing to have a growth mindset so you can learn new things to make room for the diversity in folks' identities? Yes? Then, even if you are still learning, you are doing your part.

Plus, just as identity is ever-evolving, so is all of society around it. The way to lead in the work of inclusion and equity today isn't what it was yesterday or what it will be tomorrow. It is fluid. So that means, even for those of us who are "leaders" or "experts," that if we are doing the work well, we are still learning, too. In fact, we always will be. We recognize that to make an impact on belonging, inclusion in practice has to be something that everyone can do. The more folks who role-model inclusion, the more folks will see it and begin to also role-model it.

Sometimes people are intimidated or discouraged by all the terminology that can show up in the inclusion and equity conversation – more specifically, all of the acronyms. Sometimes even I have to laugh because I can't always immediately identify all the acronyms floating around out there for what I mostly refer to as inclusion and equity work. Most recently I have heard IDEA (inclusion, diversity, and equity in action) and DEIB (diversity, equity, inclusion, and bias). Don't let all the names fool you – it is the same work. I choose to say inclusion and equity work because to me, those are the targets we are aiming to hit. Sometimes, in conversation with people in the industry, I may use the term DEI (diversity, equity, and inclusion) because it is a pretty standard term. Don't let the many acronyms and all the terminology create angst for you. There will always be new terminology. A couple of years ago folks were making the case for BIPOC (an abbreviation for Black, Indigenous, and people of color), and now in some spaces BIPOC is falling out of favor. The same is true for Latinx and Latiné (terms intended to remove gender from Latina and Latino), as some folks find those modified descriptors limiting or culturally appropriating. "Queer" was formerly considered an insult and has come into common use recently as an umbrella term for members of marginalized gender and sexuality communities. As it relates to terminology, the words and acronyms people use will change as things fall in and out of favor in society at large. You will note in this text that I use a variety of terms to be inclusive. Don't worry too much about the acronyms and terms; instead, focus on the competencies we cover from a behavior standpoint. Your goal is to behave inclusively. That means things like being open to correction (without taking offense) if you call someone

Black and they prefer African American. Or being okay with asking folks to share the proper pronunciation of their name. Or much more impactful behaviors like questioning processes in your workplace that exclude folks with disabilities or who don't speak English as their primary language. The words and acronyms will always evolve as time passes. Depending on when you are reading this book, some I use here might have evolved already. Using new words will never be progress; behaving differently is where the real progress happens.

I believe strongly in candor, so I will also share that sometimes folks like to pontificate and throw around acronyms and words to seem smart. In some cases, folks are coining whole new terms and acronyms just to get a little credit or recognition in the equity and inclusion space. It's a means of showing off – and not only is it exclusive, the reality of the situation is that someone showing off is more about them than it is about you. Don't let it intimidate you. You have a few options if someone is seeming to deliberately talk above your head: first, if you sense that you will get a respectful response, you can ask the person for clarity on the term or acronym they used. Alternatively, you can pull out your handy-dandy hand computer (i.e., your smartphone) and search for the word or acronym in question. As a final option, I cover a good amount of terminology and acronyms in my first book, *Allies and Advocates*, so you could refer to that. Generally speaking, though, it's usually worth the trouble of asking in the moment. Folks who are serious about the work of inclusion and equity will simplify because, as I said earlier, the work belongs to all of us. Just in case you encounter someone who works in inclusion and equity who is unwilling to simplify or tries to belittle you when they answer (I know it can happen), let's role-play how I recommend you manage that situation.

You ask, "What does cisgender[1] mean?"

The person you ask answers you, but adds a good amount of snark or talks to you in a tone that suggests you should already know.

You should follow up with, "Thank you for explaining. It seemed like understanding cisgender was important to me understanding the message. Should I not have asked the question?"

---

[1]Cisgender means that someone personally identifies as the same gender that was assigned to them on their birth certificate.

Most folks will adjust their temperament at that point. There is also the chance that someone might snap at you, "No, you should be doing your own research," and if that happens, respectfully end the dialogue.

It is true that you should be doing your own research, but asking questions is a healthy part of that, alongside other methods like finding information on credible websites, reading books, and learning from other leaders in the inclusion and equity space. If you are striking a balance, don't personalize someone snapping at you. Don't be compelled to continue to engage with that person anymore, either. There are many, many folks working in inclusion and equity to learn from – it doesn't have to always feel like you are being beat up – although you certainly will have moments when your ideas are challenged or you feel uncomfortable.

Bringing Inclusion to Life

Bringing inclusion to life comes down to activating three behaviors:

1. Valuing
2. Supporting
3. Connecting

In terms of being inclusive, valuing someone means that you intentionally treat them in a way that lets them know you respect them, their ideas, and whatever contribution they make. Supporting means that you are willing to give help, access, or assistance to someone because you are mindful of their needs. Connecting with someone means that you make a point to build a relationship, short or long term, and hear their perspective. None of these requires agreement or harmony. While agreeing or having a sense of harmony can help, it isn't essential. However, valuing, supporting, and connecting do require us to be respectful, intentional, mindful, and considerate.

If you think about activating valuing, supporting, and connecting carefully, you will notice that each of them is about how you engage with others. Valuing, supporting, and connecting are about the effort you are putting in to impact someone else's experience, not just your own. I notice that many of us approach inclusion with ourselves centered: "Am I included here?" That approach leaves us to stand alone in ensuring inclusion is happening to and for us. Activating inclusion is most effective when we shift away from "Am I included?" to "How does inclusion come to life for everyone here?" With this approach, if there is a room full of 20 people, instead of everyone having the mindset of watching out for themselves alone, everyone is instead being mindful about how everyone experiences feeling valued, supported, or connected. Instead of just you looking out for you, you now have you plus 20 people looking out for you. Can you imagine living in and working in a culture like that? We can get there by each being willing to shift how we bring valued, supported, and connected to life in our lives.

To be fair, valuing, supporting, and connecting are not always easy. Sometimes we have to value people who are a part of our work teams who we do not personally enjoy working with but add a lot to the team. Sometimes we have to support a direction on a project that we don't think is the best approach. Sometimes we don't automatically have a connection with someone, but we know it is important to make sure their ideas are heard by the team. Inclusion is actual labor and isn't always easy, but that is not a reason not to do the work; we all know that anything worth having often requires a bit of it.

Inclusion also is not about being nice or kind. While there are certainly times when inclusion is nice and kind, sometimes inclusion requires us to do things that are instead brave or assertive. Sometimes, however, nice or kind is not necessarily inclusive. Here is an example:

I have a dear friend who grew up in a household and a neighborhood that used a lot of homophobic language. I have talked to him about his language, and he agrees he needs to work on it, but he still – too often for my taste – says things that could be hurtful to someone who is not heterosexual. When I have people over, he cannot come to my house, because it is important to me that folks feel psychologically safe in my home. It is not nice or kind to uninvite someone from my home – but it is inclusive. Some folks have asked why I am still his friend. He is not purposely malicious, and I don't believe in throwing people away when they are actively trying to improve. There are ways I too am still growing, and I need folks to grant me the grace to grow as well.

It is important to realize that inclusion also isn't about centering everyone all of the time. Sometimes you will not be the focal point because the moment requires that someone else have the spotlight. Sometimes you will not be well represented because an organization is on the journey to shifting representation. Sometimes inclusion examples will not highlight or celebrate the specific category of uniqueness that you resonate most with. Inclusion is ever-evolving and sometimes our role in valuing, supporting, and connecting is to learn from folks with lived experience; sometimes it is to be an ally or an advocate; and sometimes it is for us to share our stories. Be open to the possibility that just because you or an identity like yours is not the focal point (sometimes called being centered) does not mean you are not included.

I know folks really like checklists. I try to avoid checklists because they suggest there is a finite way to see and experience inclusion and equity, and there is not. However, I am going to share a very light list of questions you can ask yourself if you are wondering if you are included, particularly if you are not actively centered.

- Am I welcome here?

  Welcome meaning you are gladly invited to attend and your arrival is received positively. There are times you may not feel comfortable even if you are welcome because you are not in a familiar space or with familiar people. Remember that feeling discomfort is not always a sign that you are not welcome.

- Am I physically safe?

  Physically safe means that you are not concerned about a potential threat of bodily harm by being in a space.

- Am I psychologically safe?

  Psychological safety means that you believe you can take some interpersonal risk by sharing your ideas or maybe challenging a commonly accepted perspective without damage to your reputation.

- Am I willing to consider different perspectives?

  Considering different perspectives means having an open mind when engaging in a space with others. It means staying open to the opportunity to be exposed to perspectives that are not the same as your own.

Sometimes I have clients who are White, cisgender (meaning you were born a specific gender and still identify as that gender), heterosexual men, who will say something along the lines of "I don't know if I am allowed to participate in inclusion because I am White and everyone seems upset at me." I get it. Discussions about systemic and systematic racism, oppression, and white supremacy have only continued to increase over the years. White folks can feel personally attacked and more specifically might feel like no one wants to hear what they have to share.

In reality, the opposite is true. In many cases, White folks are experiencing the kind of liberty and privilege that many other identities are seeking. If you are White, you are absolutely a part of inclusion in that, whether you know it or not, you are often the person who has the influence, power, or privilege to bring inclusion and equity to life. You often already are included, so your role, because of your identity, isn't going to be the same as the role of folks whose identities are underrepresented who are looking for access to equity you already experience. Very often your role is going to be to listen, to open doors for folks who otherwise do not have access, to unlearn behaviors that you participate in that oppress others, and to be willing to teach those you are close to how to do the same.

Remember, inclusion hasn't been "achieved" when *you* feel included. You are not the benchmark. Until *everyone* has access to being included and everyone has access to experiencing equity, there is still opportunity to improve. The journey to inclusion is a lifelong one. Sometimes what happens is we get to a point where we feel included, so we think inclusion has been achieved over all. "I was previously oppressed, and now I feel included, so everything is fine" is the energy about this. Feeling included can lead us to think that additional changes are unnecessary. Don't slip into this way of thinking. Remember that inclusion (and equity) doesn't start or end with you.

Just as a final point of note, because I often say inclusion is for everyone, occasionally I have had people ask about inclusion as it relates to ideas that are dangerous – such as pedophilia, assault, or human trafficking – and if they should still be willing to value, support, or champion those behaviors. The answer is absolutely not. Harmful things like pedophilia, assault, terrorism, or human trafficking are not things we should value, support, or champion, because they are the opposite of being intentional, mindful, and respectful of people.

3 Bias

Bias is also a buzzword and often carries a negative connotation. In my first book, *Allies and Advocates*, I explain that bias isn't really bad, and it helps us a lot. Bias, whether conscious or unconscious, is a preference, inclination, or prejudice for or against someone or something. Bias can be in favor of something or opposed to it, and there are hundreds of different bias types. Our biases are influenced by our background, cultural environment, and personal experiences. We are influenced by what we do for a living, where we went to school, where we hang out, who we are friends with, what we do for fun, and just about any of the happenings in our life. Unconscious bias just means that we aren't aware that a bias is at play. Considering that the human brain takes in 11 million bits of information every second, and we are only conscious of about 40 to 50 bits of that, there's a good chance a lot of our biases are unconscious.

Most folks really struggle with the idea that bias isn't bad because of the way we use the word in greater society. When we call someone biased, we really are usually saying they are missing some pertinent perspective or are passing unfair judgment. We tend to use the same meaning when we say data is biased or a process is biased. Sometimes, though, biases really help us – even though they are preference, inclination, or prejudice. I have a personal example.

Many years ago, a man I was in a relationship with got really sick and had to have a colonoscopy. I took him for the procedure and at the end of it, the doctor, who was a White man in what was probably his fifties, came to me in the aftercare room and said, "Are you his wife or girlfriend?" I said yes and he continued, "I need you to quickly listen to me before he wakes up and I want you to hear me very carefully: he is very sick. He needs surgery and he needs it immediately. He's a Black man, and I know he is going to say he isn't willing to have surgery. I want you to understand that it is going to be his only option to survive. You are going to have to talk to him." I felt physically frozen and all I could do was look at him blankly for a moment. I said, "If he could die, I'm sure he would have surgery." He gave me a concerned look, then said, "I am going to get this print of what I saw and give it to you so you can see what I saw." He returned and handed me a printed image of the most gnarly, gruesome thing – I had no idea what cancer looked like, but I knew that was what I was looking at on the page. It was so scary to see. As they wheeled my boyfriend into the room, I folded the paper and put it in my purse.

Moments later, my boyfriend was waking up from the colonoscopy and as he was coming out of the stupor, the doctor began to explain to my boyfriend what he saw in his colon. The doctor explained he couldn't say what it was until the biopsy came back but it was imperative that he make an appointment with a specialist and he might need to have surgery. My boyfriend, barely out of his medicated stupor, immediately snapped, "I'm not having surgery." My blood ran cold at the same time doctor looked across the room at me.

The doctor's bias told him that Black men do not get surgery. That bias made him come to me immediately, before my boyfriend came to, and warn me that I would need manage my boyfriend's temperament about having surgery in order for him to survive. I can't tell you for sure what would have happened had the doctor not talked to me or given me the piece of paper with the picture. What I know is I was so grateful that he took the few minutes before my boyfriend woke up to say something to me even though it was clearly deeply based in his own bias.

By the way: my ex-boyfriend and I are still friends and while he did indeed have a large cancerous mass in his colon, I am happy to report he did have surgery to remove it. He also celebrated being 10 years cancer free in 2020.

Bias is going to happen. We are all biasing all over everywhere all the time – and the bias in our brains isn't really a problem. Where problems could arise is the behaviors we exhibit as a result of those biases. So, for example, a bias could cause folks to treat people differently based on assumptions about their financial status or because of how they look – the different treatment could be more favorable treatment or discriminatory treatment. Either way, it is still rooted in bias.

Bias is important to accurately understand because it is happening all the time and you will never be able to turn it off. Unfortunately, there is a lot of information that suggests that you can get rid of bias – you can't. What you *can* do is work to correct discriminatory and offensive behaviors that are based on your bias. You may very well still have the biased thought run through your mind, but when you are conscious that you might offend or harm someone, you purposely work to behave differently. Sometimes you know better, but your bias still gives you the result it has formed based on past experience or information.

One of my coaching clients – let's call her Kellie – has a real bias about pronoun use. She finds it really difficult to believe that anyone can be a gender beyond the binary male or female. So, when a person joined her team who uses they/them pronouns, she continued to use binary pronouns based on how she saw their gender for a long while, until HR stepped in and advised her that she was being offensive. Kellie committed to herself to use the person's name and avoid using pronouns altogether. Not ideal or even reasonable at all.

When Kellie mentioned this in one of our coaching sessions, I shared that she has a bias. Her response was, "I just feel like I could do this if I understood; it totally doesn't make sense for someone to not use grammatically correct pronouns." I pushed, "Do you need to understand to be respectful?" She paused and I continued, "I am friends with a gay man, I do not necessarily *understand* why he or anyone would be gay, but I can still *respect* that he is gay. Is it possible that you can push past your bias of 'this is wrong' and lean into 'this is inclusive' and call your team member what they want to be called? I'd bet they don't really care if you understand as much as they just want to be respected and feel included like everyone else." Kellie thought for a moment and then agreed. A few sessions later she shared that she still has her bias and still feels strange about someone not using he or she pronouns. "It crosses my mind a lot," she shared. However, Kellie has totally found it easier to make the shift to call people what they want to be called.

In short, your bias might take a long time to shift. Your behavior, which is where problems can arise, can shift more quickly if you let go of your need to understand. Whether you understand or not should not drive your ability to be respectful and inclusive.

4 Feedback

Just about everyone I know gets a little nervy about feedback. Some folks don't know how to take it, some don't know how to give it, and others are good at one or the other. Although the word *feedback* does not carry the same level of negativity as *bias* or *privilege*, some folks see it as a challenge; I'd like to offer another perspective. Feedback, whether given or received, is an opportunity. Giving feedback is an opportunity for you to help someone learn what they are doing well or where they might have an opportunity to improve. Done well, giving feedback can also build trust, because people may grow to value knowing someone will be honest with them. Receiving feedback is an opportunity to learn what is going well and where we might be displaying some bias or have an opportunity to grow. Just look at how many times opportunity is in this paragraph. Feedback isn't bad.

Let me be clear; I do understand why folks struggle with feedback. Receiving feedback can make us feel nervous about what will be said, sometimes we don't really value or trust the source of the feedback, and occasionally the feedback might catch us off guard. Giving feedback makes folks nervous because no one is ever quite sure how someone might react to it, especially if it is not good. People also are unsure what to say when giving feedback and can be concerned that tough feedback might ruin the relationship. All of these are valid concerns. The good news is, all of them can be overcome with a shift in mindset.

Feedback helps us to be more inclusive because it gives us insight into where we can grow when we receive it and it helps others identify where they can grow when we give it. If no one ever tells us when we have offended, our ability to evolve and move closer to being inclusive and equitable is limited. If we never tell someone where they can grow, we are limiting someone's chance to evolve to be more inclusive. We won't see all of our growth opportunities in ourselves independently, or pick it all up in books we read and through our lived experiences. Also, like many things, the more you practice it, the better you get at overcoming the nerves around feedback.

Let's approach feedback the same way I covered it in *Allies and Advocates*, from two perspectives: seeking and receiving feedback, and speaking up and giving feedback.

Seek and Expect Feedback

So how do you seek feedback? Well, the best way is to ask for it from folks around you. Often people may have feedback for us, but because much of our culture in America teaches us to be nice, people will not volunteer unless you ask. If you really want to know how you are doing or how your messaging comes across or if you are being equitable – ask. An ask for feedback might sound like, "Thanks so much for your presence in the meeting. I was wondering if you would be willing to share any feedback you have for me on how I did?" Alternatively, you might say, "I am working to achieve the goals we set as a department around inclusion, but I want to be sure I am not missing anything. Is there a chance you have some feedback you'd be willing to share with me?" People don't get asked for feedback often, so you may get a number of responses saying people don't really have anything to share. That is okay. Even if someone does not have any feedback to share, you asking in a responsible way lets them know you are open to feedback so if they have some to share at another time, they are more likely to come to you.

We won't like some feedback that we receive, but allies and advocates recognize when the feedback is constructive and useful, even when it doesn't feel great. A professor friend of mine was frustrated that her past couple classes of students have had a few folks who use nonbinary pronouns and some who have changed pronouns over the semester. "Amber, I am just so frustrated and honestly it is just too much work!" I replied to her, "Now wait a moment. You sound like you are deep in your privilege! Do you not remember when you were in college and people started calling you Mike because they thought your name was too hard and they knew you were a lesbian? Do you remember crying about that?" My friend got quiet, and I continued, "Now you want to say you think it is too hard to see your students at a time when you know folks are figuring out their identities? Do you think this is different than what you went through?" Tough feedback for her to hear and some tough memories for her to relive, but so valuable. I am so grateful that she was open to the feedback and willing to hear me out. She followed up with me days later and thanked me for the perspective, even though it made her cry. She felt it was the perfect reminder to invite feedback as often as possible because you will be assisted in identifying your own biased behaviors and habits that can cause others to feel excluded or judged.

There are three main things to keep in mind when receiving feedback:

1. **Be appreciative of feedback.** Always say thank you for the feedback that people share with you, even if you are not sure you are going to use it. Thanking people lets them know you appreciate the feedback but also that you appreciate whatever emotional obstacles they may have had to overcome to share the feedback with you. Giving feedback is hard and no one owes it to you. So when you do get it, express gratitude.

2. **Avoid being defensive.** I know sometimes feedback can set us on the defense, but when we get defensive, our tone changes, our body language changes, and what could be a simple feedback discussion can turn into a conflict. When you catch yourself beginning to be defensive, remind yourself the feedback isn't personal; it is an opportunity to see another perspective. If you really are struggling to keep your composure, ask the person giving you the feedback if they would be willing to set up some time to discuss the feedback later so you can prepare yourself to listen. Make sure to honor your word, though, and follow up.

3. **Be prepared to apologize.** Occasionally we receive some feedback that lets us know we need to circle back and apologize. In fact, I encourage folks to be aware that we are living in a world with people who are having human experiences different than ours. If you are not finding opportunities to apologize, you are not leaning in enough. Missteps are going to happen. Apologizing meaningfully is a real challenge based on some of the apologies we have seen from celebrities and corporations, but it doesn't have to be hard. A meaningful apology has two parts:

- I apologize for _____.
- Moving forward I will _____.

For example:

I apologize for abbreviating your name. Moving forward I will make sure to say it correctly.

I apologize for my remarks about the upcoming Pride events. Moving forward I will mind my bias before speaking.

Simple. An apology is not conditional. It is not "I'm sorry you feel that way" or "I didn't mean to offend you." It isn't about you and how you feel, it is you recognizing you made a mistake and taking ownership of it.

Keeping these tips in mind should set you on the path to being able to lean into seeking and receiving feedback. Keep in mind, too, feedback you receive isn't always going to require action, and sometimes you will be able to disregard it. I get feedback all the time that I say thank you for and never apply because it just doesn't really fit. I still keep my heart, mind, and ears open, though, because I have also gotten feedback that has made a massive impact and I don't want to miss that by not being receptive.

Speak Up and Give Feedback

Receiving feedback is only half of the feedback loop; true allies also speak up and give feedback to others. Sometimes when it is time for us to give feedback, we get nervous, are unsure what to say, and are gripped with fear of saying the wrong thing. Push past those emotions. Speaking up and giving feedback to others is how you cultivate a culture of candor and accountability. At my company, Cabral Co., we give (and ask for) feedback constantly because we know the more we get in the habit of talking about the tough stuff, the easier it is for us to get to solve. Respectfully and responsibly giving feedback is a way to hold folks accountable for doing their best to contribute to bringing inclusion and equity to life.

Let's cover a few techniques to help you give feedback in ways that are helpful and unlikely to cause an upset.

1. **Say something when you see or hear something that is inappropriate**, especially if it is in a space you engage in frequently, like with friends, family, or in the workplace. It didn't happen to you? It doesn't matter. Allies speak up. How do you speak up? Well, it depends.

   If you want to say something subtle, try saying something like "Hmm. Can we go back a bit? I am not sure I follow what you mean by [insert what you heard]," or my personal favorite, "Can you say more about that?" We will dig into tone and body language in the next part of the book, but pour on the curiosity when you ask these questions. It keeps the encounter from going from a slight inquisitive nudge to seeming confrontational or an attempt to embarrass someone.

   Sometimes you will want to be more straightforward. Usually these are times when you see something blatantly harmful or offensive. You might say, "I find what you said inappropriate and offensive, and I'd like to share why. When is a good time for us to have a conversation?" Alternatively, you might say, "I'm not sure that is the most inclusive approach. Maybe a better approach might be [insert your suggestion]." What's really good about the second option is it uses the word *inclusion*, which we already know is a buzzword. That means it piques folks' attention and no one wants to be seen as not inclusive, so it makes the person more inclined to hear you out.

2. When it is not harmful, you don't always have to give feedback in the moment. In those times **ask for permission to share feedback** instead of blurting your thoughts all over someone. If we are going to share some perspective with someone, we want them to be in the best space to receive it, whether the message is good or bad. Asking for time to discuss allows the person you want to speak to the opportunity to emotionally prepare themselves for the discussion, which is a way of communicating respect.

3. When speaking up and giving feedback, be aware of and **use your power and privilege**. Sometimes you will find that you are able to influence decisions, impact others' behavior, and help educate folks simply by virtue of your identity or your position. If you are a White man, very often people will listen to what you

have to say simply because you are a White man. That might not feel great to hear, but rather than feeling a particular way about it, use the privilege. The same is true when you are the person who speaks the dominant language in a community, or when you have the most senior title in the room. There are lots of reasons we can have privilege, and I cover privilege in more detail in the next chapter.

I don't want to suggest that giving and receiving feedback are easy, but they are not hard, either. What feedback does is makes us feel nervous or uncomfortable because we are faced with having to talk about something we haven't had to or don't know how to discuss. Trust me, most of the time feedback is fine when it is delivered respectfully. Most of the time people are grateful to know where they can improve, even if they are uncomfortable getting the feedback in the moment. Discomfort gets in the way of a lot and it often is unfounded, which is why I talk more about it in Part III of this book. For now, though, just remember to push past the initial discomfort you have around feedback because it is really an opportunity we can benefit from.

5 Privilege

The word *privilege* conjures up some pretty nasty images or moods for many people. Maybe you hear the word and you imagine one of the well-known billionaires taking exploratory trips to space or you think of some famous socialite families. Or perhaps you are White and your shoulders tense up at the idea of being told you are privileged just because of the container your soul lives in. Maybe you are pretty financially secure and the word *privilege* sets you on the defense because, after all, you know you still worked to get where you are, or maybe you are the first in your family to have any sense of success or stability and no one cut you any breaks for you to get here. Maybe you even turn your nose up at the idea of privilege and consider yourself not to be privileged at all.

Whatever your negative perceptions or associations are with privilege, I'm going to ask you to drop them for a moment and consider another perspective. Privilege isn't bad. We think it is, because privilege, which is actually critical for us to both acknowledge and understand, has developed a negative connotation. We read about how someone's perspective "reeks of privilege" or see folks online told to "check their privilege" when they are celebrating something that not "everyone" has access to enjoy. It can feel bad to realize you have privilege and can also seem like you should feel bad about it.

None of that is true and, more importantly, none of it is useful to being an ally, an advocate, or creating inclusive spaces and communities.

The fact of the matter is two things are true about privilege:

1. We all – as in just about everyone – have some kind of privilege.
2. Most of us really struggle to see our privilege clearly because privilege, by definition, feels very typical for us.

Consider the following:

- Did you wake up this morning with hot, clean, running water?
- Do you speak the language most commonly used in your community?
- Do you have an accent that feels familiar to the folks you communicate with most often?
- Do you have typical use of your body?
- Do you think twice about the time of day or the neighborhood before refueling your vehicle or going for a walk?
- Do people generally correctly assume your gender when speaking to you?
- Are the internet, electricity, and shelter relatively accessible to you at any given moment?

Whichever experiences you said yes to in the previous list, ask yourself: Do think about those privileges as you are experiencing them? Do you feel deep gratitude each time you turn on your faucet? Do you notice that you communicate easily and often in the same language with people in your neighborhood or workplace? Do you recognize when a space is not accessible to someone whose body doesn't work like yours?

No?

That not noticing piece – that's privilege.

Privileges are rights, advantages, or protections granted or accessible to a particular person or group of people. You don't even think about it. We all have some privileges – some are earned, like financial privilege or social privilege. Others we receive just by virtue of living in the body we inhabit, or the community we reside in. Likely we don't even notice it.

Being an ally and an advocate asks us to do the labor of acknowledging and identifying our privileges. You can start to identify ways you are privileged by asking yourself the question: In what ways am I or my life typical or regular? Do you communicate easily and without cultural or language barriers with people in your community? Is your sexuality seen as typical? Did you have a pretty typical education experience?

As you begin to realize just how many things are privileges, remember that privilege is not a reason to feel bad, guilty, or ashamed, and do your best to push those emotions aside. Privilege exists and you have some.

In fact, our privilege grants us an ability to have power. If you have the privilege to have access to a quality education, or clean running water, or time to prioritize your fitness – you should enjoy those things! You should also recognize that the privileges you have not only make some aspects of your life easier, they give you the power to make an impact and be committed to determining how your privilege can make you a better ally or advocate.

Privilege is only really seen as a problem when folks don't also do the labor of recognizing it and considering how they can improve conditions for less privileged folks. For example, coming to awareness about your access to water might sound like "I'm so grateful my water is always hot, clean, and running. I know some people do not have access to that" as recognition of the privilege. The next step toward empathizing with those who have a different experience could sound like "I know the people of Flint, Michigan, didn't have clean water from 2014 to 2019. I want to better understand that crisis and how that experience has impacted the residents of Flint." As you learn more about the crisis, and develop empathy, you can begin to consider how you might extend your privilege, which could sound like "I've learned there are some organizations who are committed to holding leaders in Flint accountable for repairing the damage done to the residents during the water crisis. I'm going to donate some time or dollars to help sustain their efforts." This is moving from privileged individual to ally.

Feeling guilty can really create an obstacle to being an ally when we are confronted with our privilege. We can be so distracted by the emotion that we don't move on the opportunity. A friend's son, Jonathan, is in private swim lessons that are pretty pricy, and now that his son can swim, he and his wife are thinking it is about time to get him into a class with some other kids so he can swim socially. Well, he and his wife look into the local YMCA and find that swim classes are less than half of what they are paying now, really reasonable, but the first feeling my friend has is guilt for taking up a spot at the Y. "Should I do this? I mean, kids need swimming, and whose spot will Jonathan be taking?" After sharing his concerns with his wife about their privilege and his guilt about taking a spot from a kid who can't afford to take private lessons, his wife chimed in with an idea. "Well, how about we put Jonathan in the class and pay for another child in need to also attend? That way," she added, "he will get the social time and it will be with a diverse set of kids, too." My friend and his wife were aware of their privilege, empathized with those without the same access, and used the opportunity to extend their privilege to someone in need.

Here is another example, but this time of advocacy (which focuses on systems or processes), versus allyship (which is focused on the people):

Awareness of the privilege:
You notice that a lot of folks who are very similar to you in terms of race and life experience work at the company where you work. In fact, a lot of you even went to the same handful of schools. Maybe you also notice that there are almost no Black people at your workplace – and there were not many Black folks at the college you attended, either.

Empathize with those without the same privilege:
The next time you have a hiring opportunity on your team, you decide to have a conversation with the talent acquisition team to determine where and how they are finding candidates. You discover from your discussion that talent acquisition leans heavily on the relationships they have with the schools that are already represented well within the company. You realize that this may have an impact on the company's access to Black talent.

Use your privilege to advocate to change the system:
You work with your talent acquisition partner to source talent from a variety of places and communicate that you are looking for a candidate slate for the open role on your team that is more representative of the customers your organization is serving and would like to serve. You work to put together an inclusive job description to appeal to the candidates you are interested in and make sure to have diverse interview panels for all candidates throughout the process.

I encourage us all to do a bit more to mind our language around privilege so as not to reinforce the negative connotation that the word has picked up. Instead of "reeks of privilege," maybe say "steeped in privilege." Instead of telling folks to "check their privilege," maybe we ask a question that gets people to consider a perspective their privilege could be preventing them from seeing. To assist you, we cover asking powerful questions in Part III of this book. What we should not do is attempt to hide our privilege and only amplify stories of depravity or lack. Instead, a better approach is for us to always be open to the possibility that there is a point of view we are not seeing clearly – and yes, it could be because of privileges we have like being White, having financial security, being typically abled, the language we speak, our gender, age, or many more identifiers.

6

Allyship and Advocacy

Allyship is when someone with privilege and power (which we have covered) seeks to learn about the experiences of a marginalized group of people, develops empathy for them, and identifies ways to extend their privilege to the marginalized group. Allies are identified by their ability to apply what they have learned about a group of people and find ways to transfer the benefits of their privilege to those who lack the same access. Allyship requires taking the time to get invested in and building an emotional connection to marginalized people who are different than you – people who do not experience privilege the way you do. Allyship requires labor. An ally "seeks to learn about" – they do the labor of understanding so they can connect and build empathy. To be an ally, you have work to do: first, the labor of identifying your own privilege, then the labor of understanding a person or community of folks different than you so you can connect and build empathy. I always remind people to think of *ally* as a verb, so it only applies if you are taking action.

Advocacy is the process where someone with privilege and power (that's us) is willing to take steps to protect, advocate for, and dismantle systems against a marginalized group of people. In order to be an advocate you have to be willing to do additional work above getting familiar with the nuances of and developing empathy for a marginalized group. It is about taking action to change how others experience the world through the systems and processes. Similar to *ally*, *advocate* is not a title, but a verb.

Sometimes people put allyship on a lower tier than advocacy. That is not really accurate. Both roles are important and necessary. A simple way of distinguishing between the two is that allyship is focused on the individual or group of people and their unique experiences and perspectives, whereas advocacy is focused on systems and processes. In order to be an advocate you have to protect people from harm done by an oppressive process, and you have to be willing to dismantle systems that may serve you but are not equitable for others. Here is a simple example:

If you work for Super Retailer A and you know their processes inside and out, from how they interview to what they are looking for in candidates, and you have a friend who doesn't have the privilege to know that information, allyship would be taking some time and telling them what they need to know to prepare to ace the interview.

Now let's say you work at Super Retailer A and you notice that you seem to lose a lot of your South Asian applicants when they get to the second interview. You dig a little deeper and realize that a prerequisite for the second interview is for the applicant to write an essay. You take a look at the essay questions and notice they are not the most inclusive and also, they are not framed well for someone who is not deeply familiar with American culture. An advocate will work to get the process changed so that the essay questions are more inclusive and do not require someone to have a deep working knowledge of American culture – even if the questions work well for them.

In *Allies and Advocates* I do a deep dive into both allyship and advocacy, outlining the behaviors that are hallmarks of doing both well. If you are looking for more context on these two concepts, that book is probably a good place to start. As you read this book it may be helpful to remember that sometimes the way that you are an ally to a person is by advocating for a change in a process, which is why I try to make sure people understand you can do and be both at the same time.

7 Equity

Equity is about fairness in the way people are treated. It considers the unique needs of each person or group when determining how to treat or support someone. Equity considers that everyone does not have the same starting place and may need something different depending on their unique circumstances.

Folks struggle with equity sometimes because it requires us to consider that someone may need something we don't and if they get it, it seems like they are getting "more" or "better" than everyone else. It is usually helpful if folks have a good understanding of privilege before we start talking about equity, because then people don't see equity as someone receiving "more or better" but will more likely see it as "fair." Let's explore an example.

Imagine that you are the head of finance for a big tech corporation, and you are doing great – meeting and exceeding all the goals and projections consistently. Each year your team takes in interns and you hope to be able to extend job offers to them for employment after they graduate, but that depends on their performance over the 10-week summer program. After a couple of years you notice that the Black students are not performing as well as other students so they do not receive as many job offers, although they come from the same kinds of quality learning programs. You are concerned about this and have your team start reviewing exit survey data from previous years, looking for trends, as you are planning the upcoming summer program. One of your colleagues says to you, "I think I know what might be happening." They explain that most of the Black students don't have the same extracurricular backgrounds on their resumes as the other students. Sure, they are performing well in school and are in amazing programs, but in most cases, the internship is their first exposure to finance in a corporate environment. Many of the other students have more experience. "I think we should develop a pre-internship program," your colleague says. "We don't have to target the Black students, but we can offer all of the interns the opportunity to come a week early to learn the building, meet their mentors, and learn a bit about our company culture. It can be optional." You know the program is going to cost a bit of money because you will have to house interns who sign up for an additional week.

The equitable decision would be to offer the program. If the issue truly is that the Black students have had limited exposure to corporate culture and business opportunities, you are creating a chance for the interns who attend (not just the Black interns) to adjust before they get into the business of their summer jobs. By offering the program to every intern, you are not singling out the Black students.

Sometimes in scenarios like the one we just explored, we think of equity as charity. It isn't. It is recognizing that the playing field is not level and doing your part to set people up for success, no matter their background, if they meet your standards for quality talent. Let's talk through another scenario so you can see what I mean.

Again, you are the head of finance for a big tech corporation. Your favorite nephew, a new college graduate with a business degree, and an incredible cook, partially paid for his education by selling meals while he was in school. After graduation, he has decided he doesn't want to join a company but explore his passion for food, so he buys a food truck. There are a few food truck parks in your area, so you support his idea and offer to help him, including planning his finances. You see it as a great entrepreneurial way to use his degree.

The first few months with the food truck are great. Your nephew is making a little money and even has a few lunchtime regulars, which is when he makes the bulk of his cash. You have only visited the food truck a couple of times, but you talk to him on the phone regularly to see how things are going.

Well, a small personal matter arises that requires your nephew to be away from the food truck for about a week and, as a new food truck, he is worried about losing loyal customers. Since you've been along for the journey, you offer to take some time off work and cover for the week to help him out. Your nephew is hesitant, saying, "That's asking a lot. I am not sure you know the business," but you assure him that you know business and have been doing well at it for a long time. You are confident that with a little direction, you should be able to pick up the essentials pretty quickly. Your nephew agrees to let you help and he walks you through the essentials over the next couple of days before he has to leave. You shadow him for a day and ultimately feel good about your knowledge of the business when your nephew boards his flight to go take care of the personal matter.

You start the next day setting up the food truck and doing all the things that your nephew told you to do. Business is slow the first day. A few potential customers pop over and ask where your nephew is and you let them know he will be back the following week, and most of them walk away without ordering. You try again the next day and things are even worse, and you've done everything your nephew told you, so you don't get what is happening. By the third day, you mention to your nephew things aren't going so well. He gets worried and walks through all the procedures, which you both agree you are following. Finally, he says, "How are you engaging with folks? You know, connecting with them." You are confused. "I say hello, welcome them, and I ask how I can help." "Ah," he says. "It's more to it than that; food is love. People have to pick up that you are excited about the food."

Now, your nephew technically gave you everything you needed to run the food truck, but what he didn't give you was an understanding of the culture around the food truck community – how he engages with customers, the way he talks about his food, and the passion he exudes when he is serving someone. In fact, he can't really give you that; you have to learn it by being around. So, in this scenario, you, a corporate businessperson, need a little more to be successful. You probably could have used a few more days shadowing your nephew and paying attention to how he behaves with people. Another food truck person might have picked that up right away, but you need an equitable onboarding where you learn about food truck culture so you can make the same level of impact.

Equity is not charity or pity or someone getting more or better. It is looking at someone's starting place and giving them what they need to be successful. As my dear friend Ifeoma (Ify) Ike, founder and CEO of Pink Cornrows and founder of Black Policy Lab, writes in her LinkedIn article titled "'I Won't Be the Last': The Equity Message You Shouldn't Miss in VP-Elect Kamala Harris' Speech," "Equity is only achieved via awareness of truth, declaration of that truth, and a commitment to act in light of that truth."[1] The truth is, representation and visibility are nice, but without equity, they won't mean much. People won't stay. Folks can't thrive. And ultimately, they, and you, will, often bitterly, move on. Privilege is real. Some of us have access to information, resources, and opportunities that the rest of us do not. As long as that is the case, there will be a need for equity.

Equity is small things, too, like making sure that a wheelchair user's access to a hotel and all its amenities is the same as those for a person who has typical use of their legs. It is adding braille to ATM buttons. It's offering gender options on passports and driver licenses beyond the binary male and female. Things that are not always grand gestures or large programs but go a long way in creating a sense of belonging for someone – that is equity. Inclusion only happens when there is equity. This is why some leaders and organizations have decided to add equity to their goals alongside diversity and inclusion.

Now that we have reviewed the concepts and terms I use the most frequently in this book, you should have a better understanding of the terminology and concepts that might come up when you are pushing back or speaking up. Most of our lives come down to a series of moments when we are seeking inclusion and equity for ourselves or for others. I hope this part of the book helped to bring that point to life and also to arm you with some perspectives that will make navigating conversations easier as you continue on our journey toward a more inclusive and equitable experience for everyone.

---

[1]Ifeoma Ike, Esq., "The Equity Message You Shouldn't Miss in VP-Elect Kamala Harris' Speech," https://www.linkedin.com/pulse/i-wont-last-equity-message-you-shouldnt-miss-vp-elect-ike-esq-/.

Understanding the Landscape

Now that we have reviewed the concepts and terms I use most frequently in this book, let's examine the landscape that we are encountering as we speak up. In this section of the book, I revisit those obstacles we talked about in the Introduction – understanding, accountability, fear, discomfort, and time – and give you some support and tools on how to overcome them. I also get into culture here, specifically American culture, but I touch on some ethnic cultural elements so you get an understanding on the part these can play when we come face to face with needing to speak up. I also want to give you a little inspiration that you can use when you need to dig a little deeper to find the resilience necessary to push back when you are feeling a bit nervy about it.

Before digging into this landscape section, I want to say something you may have already gathered while reading through Part I. The work of inclusion and equity is nuanced and very subjective, just like people, because it is about people's experiences. As a result, there are no universals, and it is imperative that the work is ever evolving – also just like people.

I know most of us really enjoy some stabilities and consistency in our experiences and associate them with things being mostly static. Try your best not to see the evolutionary nature of the work of equity and inclusion as a bad thing. Instead, see the value in the consistency of staying open to learning, growing, and making space for the multitudes of identities we will encounter throughout our lives. We are all different. We also have a ton of commonalities. Inclusion and equity are asking us to remember just as we are all individually evolving, so too is everyone else and to practice giving space and grace to all of that.

Now, about those obstacles . . .

8 Overcoming the Most Common Obstacles

In the Introduction, I mentioned five common obstacles that get in the way of people speaking up. To revisit, they are:

1. Understanding: This might sound like "I don't know if I understand/agree/believe that disabled people face discrimination, so I am just going to be quiet."
2. Accountability: This might sound like "I don't think my leader understands/agrees/believes in inclusion, I think they are just checking the box and I don't know how to hold them accountable."
3. Fear: This might sound like "I am afraid to say something in case it is the wrong thing to say."
4. Discomfort: This might sound like "I am uncomfortable talking about racial equity." Or it can sound like "I am afraid of making others uncomfortable by addressing inequitable behaviors."
5. Time: This might sound like "I don't have the time to correct every single person I encounter." Or it can sound like "We are moving so quickly, I don't have the time to be inclusive."

We cover a lot of other things in this part of the book that can get in the way of us speaking up, from cultural impact, to trauma, to challenges with confidence, but these five are the ones I hear the most frequently, and they are honestly the easiest to work on, so let's start here.

Understanding

Most folks want to reach a certain level of understanding about something before they are willing to engage. We want to understand what our workplace meetings are about. We want to understand our family dynamics. In seeking understanding, we are also often looking to agree or approve of things. I understand what this meeting is about, so I can agree to attend. I understand my family dynamics, so I know what family events I will agree to attend and which I will not. When we encounter a perspective that we do not understand or a point of view that does not align with what we see as the "right" way, sometimes we elect to disengage and ignore the point of view. We might decide we are not going to respect the perspective or we might even belittle it.

For example, some folks do not understand rap music and have therefore decided that all of it is terrible, it isn't real music, and rap artists don't deserve any credibility or attention. Those folks may even feel that rap artists aren't artists at all, simply because they cannot relate or because the music doesn't resonate with them.

Another example is when folks say something like "I don't understand how someone can be transsexual, because sex is something we are all born into." As a result of this perspective, that person treats everyone they encounter as the gender identity they see, regardless of how the person they are interacting with may regard themselves – which is disrespectful and ignores a part of a trans person's identity. Alternatively, some folks may elect to disengage and ignore a trans person altogether.

Occasionally, instead of understanding and agreement, the sentiment is belief. For example, "I believe it is a sin to get a divorce" or "I believe it is a sin to eat pork." Understanding, agreement, and belief are personal aspirations and occasionally excuses for not engaging, but they are not real obstacles.

Your understanding, agreement, or belief is not essential to you being inclusive. It is possible and reasonable not to understand someone being transgender and still treat them inclusively, equitably, and with respect. It is possible and reasonable to believe it is a sin to get divorced and still treat a divorced person inclusively, equitably, and with respect. It is possible and reasonable not to agree that rap music is real music and still treat rappers inclusively, equitably, and with respect.

It might be nice if someone did not eat pork because you think it is a sin, but what someone else eats should not be a reason you cannot treat them inclusively, equitably, and with respect. Sure it would be nice to understand why someone would eat pork, and perhaps by leaning into your growth mindset, one day you will understand, but understanding is not critical for your behavior to change. You can decide right now that you are going to treat someone inclusively and equitably even if they do some things you do not understand, agree with, or believe in.

Consider for a moment: Do you want folks to exclude you from opportunities, to treat you dismissively, or be disrespectful to you because they don't agree with your beliefs? How would you like it if people called you by the name they felt best suited you instead of the name you shared with them? Imagine if folks decided not to speak to you because they didn't like or understand your accent.

So many of us mistreat people we don't understand or who believe differently than us all the time, even unknowingly. We avoid making eye contact with the Black man in the airport who has face tattoos. We try not to cross paths with the trans person who sits a couple of rows over from us in the office. We try not to ride the elevator with the sight-impaired woman who uses the white cane to navigate. We feel nervous when we notice a man wearing a turban boarding our flight. We don't understand, or we don't agree with, or we believe differently, so we disrespect, avoid, or disconnect instead of leaning in to be inclusive, equitable, and respectful. Making understanding, agreement, or shared beliefs a prerequisite for inclusion is not allyship or advocacy.

Practice letting go of your need to understand, agree, or believe the same as everyone around you for you to engage with them. These desires are personal to you and they should not impact how you behave toward people. Holding on to the requirement of understanding, agreement, or shared beliefs does nothing but limit your experience of people to only those who are a lot like you. How is that inclusive? It isn't.

You don't have to adopt someone's ideology to get to know them. You don't have to become a thing to make room for it to exist. Inclusion is not asking for your understanding or your belief. It is asking for your willingness to be exposed to difference and grant it the same safety you want for yourself. Start moving past your need to understand or align beliefs and you might be surprised at how your exposure to the uniqueness in others might evolve your existing understanding and beliefs.

A Note About Binary Thinking

A great many things are on a spectrum, but we humans tend to enjoy our binary options. Yes or no. Male or female. Love it or hate it. Hot or cold. Tall or short. Republican or Democrat. Foreign or domestic. Pro-choice or pro-life. As a general matter, a binary perspective can be obstructive to being inclusive; try to be open to there being another perspective you might not have considered. Maybe the answer isn't yes, but it is not no. Maybe I don't love it, but I don't really hate it either. The English language doesn't lend itself very well to the messy middle, but I'd bet more of us land there in a lot more cases than folks actually realize.

I had a friend ask me how I enjoyed my Halloween. I replied, "I honestly largely forgot it was Halloween. I don't enjoy the holiday." Their reaction was, "Oh, why don't you like Halloween?" I replied, "I didn't say I don't like Halloween. I don't dislike it, I just don't delight in it either. It happens and if there happens to be a way for me to indulge and I want to, I will. Otherwise, it can kind of come and go easily for me." "Oh," they said, "so more like you aren't festive about it." I paused, because I do totally have a little Halloween decor up in my home, but I said, "Sure. That's close enough, I guess. I don't like horror, but I would totally take kids trick-or-treating."

Do you see how hard it was for us to get to the space where we understood the same thing? Since it wasn't squarely in the presented binary perspectives of "like Halloween" or "dislike Halloween," we had to bat the idea around a bit to land in a space where we were close to a common understanding. Did you notice how their statements tried to force me into a binary perspective when I said, "I don't enjoy the holiday"? They immediately went to "Why don't you like it?"

I don't expect that humans will evolve from binary thinking easily because it simplifies a lot, but life and grander society is asking us to try. Maybe in the future, instead of hearing my "I do not enjoy Halloween" as "she dislikes Halloween," folks will instead lean into trying to understand with questions like, "Oh, what don't you enjoy about it? Is there anything about Halloween that you do enjoy?"

None of this is unique to any specific group of folks – it is not just binary pronoun users or White people or folks who have really traditional identities. Collectively, we all really struggle reacting to things that are not proximate to ourselves and how we live and see life. So we lean first to simplify, which leads to binary thinking, when we could instead lean into being curious.

Accountability

Another obstacle to bringing inclusion and equity to life is that most of us do not hold people accountable to behaving inclusively and equitably. Sometimes we don't hold people accountable because we do not know what to say to do that. That is, we do not think people are bought in to the idea that inclusion really matters. We think they are just "touting the company line" about inclusion being central to their values, but they don't believe any of it. I can't tell you how many ways these conflicts have arisen in conversations with friends, colleagues, and coaching clients. The sentiments can sound a little like this:

- "I just don't think my leader really cares about inclusion."
- "We talk about inclusive leaders but I don't think anyone really understand what that means."
- "We have equity as a part of our values, but I'm not sure folks are bought in."
- "I think people care about not offending anyone, but I don't think they are ready to move past the performative."

I have a little secret for you: as long as the CEO and their directs are on board, it really doesn't matter if most of the other folks are bought in. I know some of you are saying "What?" but hear me out. When the top layer of leadership sets the strategy and direction for a company and those leaders have decided that inclusion matters, the rest of the organization falls in line to deliver on the strategy. Each department lead and all the leaders beneath them begin finding ways to make inclusion a part of their strategy. Admittedly, a lot of organizations are not doing this well or are doing small performative actions (which I cover later in this book), but when inclusion is a part of the company's values, the great thing is that you get to ask questions to hold folks accountable for delivering against the objective. It doesn't matter if this or that leader believes in inclusion or not, if the CEO has made it a part of the organization's goals, the business leaders across the company are going to work on it. An organization with a commitment to inclusion that they are openly speaking about means you have license to ask questions. Let me share an example:

Shauna, a friend of mine, worked on the HR team for a large tech company. She was excited to see that the company had adopted inclusion as a part of the company values and was eager to see how her leadership was going to take action on it. A few weeks later, her leaders announced in a team meeting that they were taking donations to give to a local disability charity, "to support our new commitment to inclusion." Shawna was frustrated because while she liked the idea of supporting an outside organization in need, she wasn't seeing how there was an impact being made in the company on inclusion. The next several meetings, she noticed her leaders would say things like "In alignment with our organization's goal to be more inclusive ..." and "as we strive toward a greater sense of belonging," but she wasn't seeing any real change. Shauna was frustrated when she mentioned what was happening to me during a call one day.

I asked, "Have you asked your leaders any accountability questions?" She said, "I think so," and detailed how she was making a point to call out opportunities to be more inclusive when she saw them in meetings and working to make sure she role-modeled inclusive behaviors with her team. "I still just am not sure that folks in my department are bought in," she expressed. I shared with her that role-modeling and suggesting tactics are good starting actions, but sometimes we need to use accountability questions to get things moving forward. Accountability questions do not require someone to be "bought in"; instead, they are framed in a way to remind folks of the commitments they have made to deliver for the organization. The key to a good accountability question is making sure you have paid attention to the commitments leaders or people in your life have made; then you can frame accountability questions around them.

Here are a few examples of accountability questions:

- "I know we have a commitment to be more inclusive in our department; can you share how that is coming to life on our team?"
- "I have a meeting with another team and I would like to be able to share how we are creating a sense of belonging in our department. What are some ways you would say we are making an impact?"
- "We've been talking a lot about being more inclusive. How does inclusion show up in this project/process/product, and so forth?"
- "I've heard you mention how important inclusion is to you. I'd like to hear more about that and how you are taking action."

All of these questions are valid and connect directly to the mission, vision, and values of the organization as the leaders have expressed them. When folks really mean what they have said, they might appreciate you asking them to share more. Simultaneously, folks may not enjoy being asked these questions if they are mostly saying the right things but not doing much. In either case, asked the right way, they hold folks accountable and you get a sense of whether they are acting and speaking consistently.

Here's the thing – it doesn't matter if they meant it, they said it and the organization has it as a goal. That gives you the opportunity to ask about it. Don't get upset or hype yourself up about it. You can just ask, and you asking a question doesn't have to be snarky. Your questions can be curious, which any department working toward their goal of inclusion would welcome. Even if they do not mean it, they aren't going to say that. Instead they are going to give you something you can react to that will help move you toward the goal.

So let's role-play this out in a few layers so you understand that it is not just the initial question you ask to hold folks accountable, it is the initial question plus the continued framing that forces folks to be accountable. Let's explore an example:

YOU: I know we have a commitment to be more inclusive in our department; can you share how that is coming to life on our team?

LEADER: Sure, we are making sure that we are shifting our behaviors to become a more inclusive culture and activating inclusion in our department.

YOU: I'm so excited about that! What are some examples of some behavior shifts we have seen since beginning this work or some that are in progress?

LEADER: We are becoming more respectful and inclusive communicators.

YOU: That's so important. Can you share a specific example of inclusive communication? I know there are other teams working on this and I would love to be able to share with them the great changes we are making.

Don't ever get angry, but also don't let folks off the hook. Keep your genuinely excited energy (because remember, you are excited and eager about bringing inclusion to life) and keep asking strategic questions. The heat may go up, and you may sense that the leader is getting frustrated, but keep your same kind and inquisitive energy. Usually the end of an exchange like this goes one of two ways:

1. The leader turns the table and says something like, "I would love to hear your contributions for how we can bring inclusion to life in our department/team/organization," which you can respond to with your ideas, if you have any. If you don't, you can always say something like, "I'd love to share some ideas for this team."

2. The leader says, "I'm not sure I am the right person to get into the details on this, maybe you should talk to [insert person here]." If this happens you can say something like, "Oh great! I'm happy to do that. Is there an ideal way you think I should approach the conversation?" Again, inclusion belongs to everyone. You get to ask.

Occasionally you will get a leader who will get really direct with you and they will drop their professional mask and try to get you to do the same. That might sound something like:

- "Okay, I get it, you want to highlight that we aren't doing enough. Point taken."
- "What are you trying to get to here?"
- "I see what you are doing; what do you want me to say?"

Your response to the tactic of a leader dropping their professionalism should be confusion. Say something like, "My apologies for miscommunicating; I wasn't trying to make a point, I was hoping for a response because we have been talking about this for a while." If appropriate, it might be a good time to also add in a recommendation. Something like, "I know bringing inclusion to life is challenging; I have some recommendations and ideas to help get the ball rolling. Can I share them with you?" Use your judgment here, but if the person is angry, your question will probably be received as confrontation, so I would hold off on sharing ideas until another time.

I know it might feel good to finally feel like you know what to say and, moreover, to see someone admit they are struggling with inclusion instead of making minimal impact. It might even bring you some degree of joy to have a leader drop their professionalism to get really candid with you. Just remember that feeling isn't the goal. The goal is to bring inclusion to life. Always prioritize getting inclusion on the table for real discussion so you can start making meaningful impact. Remember that shifting our culture and changing our behaviors around inclusion and equity make it clear that they are important and that we will pay attention to them in our organization. Over time, just like anything else that is important, folks will prioritize them. Folks will get on board and join the movement and folks who don't agree will eventually leave.

One final note is that tone is super important when you are strategically challenging, especially when you think someone is not serious and they are just trying to check the box. We talk about the importance of using the right tone and approach when you are challenging someone a little later in this part of the book.

Fear

I give a lot of talks about what gets in the way of folks speaking up, and fear always comes up. Fear that no one really wants to hear what we have to say. Fear of being judged by the audience. Fear of damage to one's reputation. Fear of being the only one who speaks up. Fear of being wrong. Fear is a real silencer for people, especially when they are in some way the only in the room: the only woman, the only Black person, the only gay person, the only one with a visible disability. If there happens to be someone who represents multiple underrepresented identities, like the only Black trans woman in the room – these folks can feel like speaking up for any reason is a risk and opt out entirely. Naturally, humans inherently open up so much more when they are aware they are represented. That is a big part of why a lot of leaders in the equity and inclusion space talk a lot about representation. It is not just that people aren't getting equitable access and opportunity, it is also that when there isn't representation, people are fearful of sharing their thoughts and ideas. In fact there is data from Coqual, formerly the Center for Talent Innovation, that says employees at diverse companies are 75 percent more likely to see their ideas move through the pipeline and make it to the marketplace.[1] Additionally, Coqual determined that respondents that had high belonging scores are far more likely to have senior leaders with whom they have a lot in common, or who serve as role-models for them.[2] Fear isn't really false evidence appearing real; it is indeed evidenced by data.

That said, fear can be overcome, even when you are the only in your identity in the room. Let's talk through some considerations to help you overcome the fear of speaking up.

---

[1]Sylvia Ann Hewlett, Melinda Marshall, and Laura Sherbin with Tara Gonsalves, "Innovation, Diversity and Market Growth," Center for Talent Innovation, 2013.

[2]"The Power of Belonging: What It Is and Why It Matters for Today's Workplace," Center for Talent Innovation, 2020.

When folks tell me they are afraid, the very first thing I ask them to do is to consider what happens if you say or do nothing. Is anyone hurt by your silence? Who? Does anything change for the better or worse if you speak up? Is your silence worth it? I think it is important to ask these questions of ourselves because fear is such a powerful emotion that if we don't question it, we simply react without any thoughtfulness about the repercussions.

I had a moment to consider these questions while I was in Riviera Maya, Mexico, on vacation in 2020. There was a pandemic and I had done a lot of research to find a place I could safely go on vacation. After losing 20-plus folks to coronavirus, and managing the massive influx of work that came as a result of companies leaning into racial justice and equity after George Floyd's very-well-publicized murder, I was on the edge of burnout and really needed to recharge. I opted out of most activities due to safety concerns, but I did decide that I wanted to go on the catamaran excursion during my time on vacation. I asked all the questions about mask use to ensure that I would feel safe. My main concern was the seven-minute ride to the boat dock where I would be in the van with strangers, and I was assured that masks were required for the short ride and the windows would be open. Well, the time came to go to the dock and I intentionally stood in line last to see if mask use was happening before I got in the van with the other guests. I was watching all kinds of mask use – some folks had it on properly, some had it hanging around their chin, some had their mouths covered and their noses sticking out. Since I was the last one, once the driver, who was wearing his mask correctly checked my name off, he walked around to get in the driver's seat, leaving me to get into the van with the other guests. I was uncomfortable. It was also very obvious to me that I was the only single person and I was also the only Black woman going on the trip. My friend and his boyfriend, both Black men, were with me and they were in the van already with their masks on properly. I started toward the van but I stopped short of getting in and quickly asked myself the questions I listed earlier:

- What happens if I say or do nothing? *I could get coronavirus if I say nothing.*
- Is anyone hurt by my silence? *Maybe.* If so, who? *Potentially everyone in this van.*

- Does anything change for the better or worse if I speak up? *Yes, people can put their masks on.*
- Is my silence worth it? *It is not.*

I adjusted my mask and I said, "Hey, y'all! Are we able to commit to proper mask use for 10 minutes while we ride to the dock?" Everyone in the van immediately adjusted their masks and there were "Oh, sure," remarks as they did so. Relieved, I climbed into the van and yelled "Thank you," and safely off to the docks we went. Was it easy for me to speak up? Not really, but it was worth it.

Going back to being the only in the room – when you are part of an underrepresented identity, it is very hard to say something because we get nervous about sticking out in any way that might cause people to judge us or reinforce stereotypes others may have about our identity. So if you are a Latina, you may be cautious of coming across as too sassy. If you are a tall Black man, you might be cautious about coming across as intimidating or threatening. I am a Black woman and I am cautious about coming across as angry. The stereotypes about us and members of our cultural communities can cause us to shrink or blend in because not only do we not want to reinforce a judgment or stereotype, we also might be thinking that by purposely being different we are interrupting the judgment or stereotype.

My friend, Brandon, and I stopped at a Starbucks™ in a mall one day while we were doing our shopping. While my drink is an occasional treat, he is a true coffee lover and has a specific order he likes from Starbucks™. We placed our drink orders and chatted while we waited. They said his name and he collected his drink. We were still waiting for mine as I watched him take a sip of his drink, make a face, and then examine the cup to check the order. "It's not right, is it?" I say. "It's fine," he said. I said, "No it's not, I can tell, you should say something." He looked at me for a moment in shock and said "Me? The six-foot-four, 240-pound, Black man in the room?" I replied, "Ah. I get that and I see what's happening. Let's discuss, but I am going to say something."

I called the barista over and let her know his drink was not correct. She apologized and looked to him to confirm the order, so Brandon leaned in and explained what was wrong. She remade the drink, and we continued on with our day.

As I shared with Brandon after we got our coffees, even when you are the only or are concerned about the way someone might perceive you, it is incredibly important that you speak up. First, by not speaking up, you are settling for something you didn't want and perhaps paid for. Additionally, you are not countering any stereotypes when you slink to the safety of silence. If someone has a bias about someone's identity, they mostly notice the people who reinforce it, not the casual encounters that do not. I ultimately gave Brandon some tips on how to speak up when he is concerned that someone might have some stereotypes about his identity that he is worried about reinforcing. I will share the advice I gave to him in Part III of this book in Chapter 21, Underrepresented: What If I Am the Only One?, where we cover scripts to address specific kinds of circumstances that can keep us quiet.

Sometimes folks fear speaking up because they think no one in the room wants to hear what they have to say. It is important to remember that you really never know what folks want to hear, but if you are in the room, you should assume you are there because you have something to contribute. The best thing you can do to overcome this is to prepare and then speak up and share your perspective. Consider for a moment: How long have you been hearing things like "We need more representation" or "We need more diversity in the rooms where decisions are being made"? I've been in the inclusion and diversity space for more than 20 years and the representation topic has been a discussion for at least that long. It has been amplified in recent years as employers have gotten better tracking and the job market has been pressing corporations to share more transparently. You've heard the sentiments before: We've got to get more women at the table, or more LGBTQIA+ folks at the table, or more disabled folks at the table, and so forth. Then folks get to the table and are too fearful to say anything! Yikes! Feeling psychologically safe to speak up is important, and I talk about psychological safety in a moment, but always remember that being heard and having the opportunity to speak is what many who have come before you have been asking for, so seize the moment!

The final way that fear shows up that I cover here is fear of retaliation. Many of us want to say something but are afraid that it is going to cause someone to retaliate against us or damage our reputation. Some people even reference cancel culture as an example of the kinds of retaliation that can happen. How you say things, meaning your wording, approach, and tone, can go a long way toward reducing this risk. Speaking to cancel culture specifically, most folks who have to deal with that double down on poor behaviors or they have the kind of high profile that their behavior is held to a higher standard. Likely, cancel culture is nothing for you to be concerned about. But I want to be clear – you may still find yourself in some situations where you have to weigh the risks or benefits of being honest in your situation. Based on lived experiences or the stories you have heard, you may judge it as too high a risk. My hope, though, is that at least some of the time, by leveraging the skills in Part II and the language in Part III, you will determine that you can mitigate a good amount of the risk and be able to impart some benefit to yourself and/or others.

If the content of the past few paragraphs on fear resonated for you, great! Depending on your identity and your relationship and access to opportunity, some of these paragraphs under Fear might have seemed a little strange to you, and that's okay, too. You may have felt challenged by the idea that folks don't feel like they have safe spaces to speak up; it might be because it is not a part of your lived experience. Instead of doubting whether it is fact that some folks don't feel safe or know how to speak up, consider why you do. What gives you the privilege and power to speak up? Is there an opportunity for you to be an ally and extend that privilege to others? We need you! Speaking up isn't just on the shoulders of the folks who have fear around doing it; it is also on the folks in the room who don't have fear to help make the environment an inviting one for everyone.

It is also a possibility that you are clear about your privilege and power but are still finding it difficult to connect with folks and create safe spaces for people to speak up. Here is a tip from my friend Ifeoma Ike of Pink Cornrows: "Before you say 'this is a safe space,' pause. Consider using instead 'What would make this space safe for you?' Dominant spaces that declare default safety without guidance from those harmed are far from safe." Safe spaces have to be created by inviting people to share what will make them feel comfortable. You can ask folk individually or in small team meetings about what makes spaces safe for them so you know what needs to happen to truly help eradicate fear. Remember, just because you are comfortable and safe speaking up doesn't mean a space is safe for everyone.

A Note About Tokenism

Tokenism is the act of doing something or giving visibility to someone to prevent criticism or give the appearance of inclusion or equity. An example is hiring a Native American executive vice president and making sure he is very visible to avoid criticism that the leadership team is all White. The person who is the token may or may not know they are being tokenized. People who are in a token position may have a fear of speaking up and losing the favor they have as a result of their position. Sometimes they will even lean into being celebrated as the "person of color" (or whatever identifier is being tokenized) on the team instead of seeking opportunities to create a more inclusive and equitable environment. People who are tokenized often need allies and advocates to help create a sense of safety for them to speak up.

If you find yourself as a token on a team, look for colleagues who can serve as allies and advocates on your team. Being tokenized can be hard to overcome individually without offending folks and potentially doing damage to your reputation. Build a relationship with allies so you can share your experiences and they can start to learn how they can step in and support you when you need it instead of you feeling like you are jeopardizing your position or credibility if you speak up. If you are in a role where you cannot find any allies or at an organization where the culture is not willing to adjust to be more inclusive or equitable, unfortunately, that means you will need to do what you can to survive in the role or find an opportunity with a more inclusive company elsewhere. Keep in mind that often people do not realize they are tokenizing someone until they are told. Be prepared for the possibility that you will need to explain your experiences, so allies know how to step in. Tokenism is covered in more detail in my first book, *Allies and Advocates*.

If you are on a team and you notice that someone is being tokenized, there is an opportunity for you to serve as an ally or an advocate for them. Pay attention to how they are positioned or represented on the team, for example, "our new Black head of sales" instead of "our new head of sales." If you notice tokenism happening, speak to the person who is being tokenized and build a relationship, especially if you are a member of the identity well represented on the team. As you build a relationship, you should begin to learn the best ways to support as an ally and an advocate so they do not continue to be tokenized by other colleagues.

Discomfort

Oh, humans. We are so deeply attached to comfort. We will do anything to avoid discomfort. As soon as we get that funny feeling that happens between our nose and our navel, lots of us disengage and get quiet. The funny thing about that to me is that most of us acknowledge that our most impactful life and growth moments arose out of discomfort. We even have a saying about it that we throw around: "Growth comes from discomfort," and it is true.

I mean, consider for a moment: Were you comfortable in 2020? Most of us were certainly not. But if you take a moment and look back over all the things that have happened between then and now, did you grow? Most of us grew a lot. The year 2020 was life changing and uncomfortable as we were all scrambling to figure out how to navigate the fallout of a global pandemic. We were worried about jobs; some of us even lost employment or had to severely change how we were working. Our children, big and small, were suddenly forced to figure out remote learning. We were panicked about finding disinfectant and masks and toilet paper! Then, right as we started to think we were getting a handle on things, the United States broke out into Black Lives Matter protests in response to Minneapolis Police Officer Derrick Chauvin murdering a Black man named George Floyd by kneeling on his neck for over nine minutes. In the months to follow there were protests and political unrest, not just in the United States but around the globe – all while we were trying to survive a global pandemic. Almost everyone was uncomfortable.

Yet, we grew. Out of discomfort came new ways to get many jobs done, and new hobbies. We learned how to manage home school for kids and remote learning for ourselves and our college students. We started to have bold conversations in the United States that hadn't happened since the Civil Rights Movement of the 1960s where we talked about racism, oppression, discrimination, and ways to address those things in meaningful ways in workplaces, in communities, and even on our evening news. We stretched – some of us in powerful personal ways, reconnecting with family members, even virtually, who we hadn't had time for previously. Some of us left big cities for suburbs. Some of us started small businesses. Some folks reconnected with their spouses and some fell in love. In our discomfort we grew. I grew. My business grew. I wrote my first book. I hired my first few team members. I moved back to a city I love. I was uncomfortable and lonely and frustrated and hadn't seen the people I love in months because they are older and I did not want to chance bringing them coronavirus. I lost people – people who held my world together. Yet, deep in my discomfort, I grew. So did you.

Discomfort will happen. It will feel difficult to speak up. You will be nervous about saying the wrong thing. You will think and rethink the words. All of that is okay. Say it. Do it. Try. Inclusion and equity work is connected to identity so it is emotional and can feel touchy sometimes. That is normal. Is there a possibility that someone will be offended? Absolutely. Is there a chance someone might disagree with you? Surely. What you know for sure so far, though, is that on the other side of discomfort is growth and learning. You also have tools to help you in the journey. You know how to apologize when you misstep in your communication. You know how to ask accountability questions. You know how to give and receive feedback, and we still have several chapters of learning material to go to further equip you. Practice pushing the discomfort aside because otherwise things stay the same and we don't grow. There are so many allies who say they want to see change, for themselves and for others, but discomfort keeps them playing the part of keeping things the same by not pushing past the difficulty of speaking up to share their perspectives.

The other thing about discomfort is that we avoid doing things because they feel uncomfortable, but just consider how often we do something anyway and it works out just fine. We have made up all these stories in our head about what might go wrong or how hard it will be, and very often we find that none of that happens. So when you get that nervous feeling about pushing back, remind yourself that change causes discomfort. It doesn't mean something bad is going to happen; it might just be that it is time to make some changes.

In the inclusion and equity space I also see people prioritizing the comfort of other folks. We hesitate to address poor behavior because we are prioritizing the comfort of others. On the journey to equity and inclusion, everyone is going to have to get uncomfortable. For us to grow, discomfort can't be a burden a few secretly and silently carry; it has to be something we all have a stake in working through so we can grow. That said, if you haven't yet leaned into discomfort, you should prioritize doing so. We will all go through lots of changes in our lives. We're never the same after them, but we learn to adapt. Everything is always evolving, and equity and inclusion work is no exception. If you are feeling new discomfort, that likely means you are finally doing it right.

Time

I hear so many folks say things like "Inclusion takes so much time" or "I'm so busy, I don't have time to focus on equity." Guess what? You don't need more time. Being inclusive and equitable is not a list of tasks you need to make additional time for to complete. Being inclusive and equitable is about looking at what you are doing currently and doing it more inclusively. That doesn't take more time as much as it takes intentional behaviors, mindfulness, respect, and consideration of others in the things you are already doing. If you are a parent, you are already parenting; your goal is to be a more inclusive and equitable parent. If you are a designer, you are already designing; your goal is to be a more inclusive and equitable designer. If you are a recruiter, a teacher, whatever you do – the way you bring inclusion to life is to embed it in your regular life.

Now, the things you are currently doing will perhaps feel a bit more challenging for you as you embed the practice of being equitable in your life. Just like anything else new that you are learning, you move a little slower until you are practiced. So in that sense, you may need to spend a bit more time to accomplish what you normally do because for a while your pace may be slower.

Your next thought is probably, "How do I embed inclusion into what I am doing already?" There are two questions you can start to ask yourself to think about what you are doing differently:

1. How does inclusion and equity come to life here?
2. How might this process/product/project/etc. be perceived by someone who is different from me?

These questions are the ones I ask myself regularly. They are a part of my personal routine and you can make them a part of yours too. The second one is especially valuable because you get to think about things from different perspectives – both perspectives you agree with and those you don't. Asking myself how a process/product/project/etc. might be perceived by someone who is different from me has helped me to be more inclusive in whatever I am creating and also to prepare for challenges that might arise from folks who might not feel included.

I am the chairwoman for an organization called Brown Girls Do Ballet™ and, as the name suggests, our focus is on girls and young women. I am often asked whether we have a branch for boys and I am prepared for this because I have asked myself, "How might this process/product/project/etc. be perceived by someone who is different from me?" many times. The answer is that we would love to support boys and young men, but at this time, we do not have the funds or capacity as a nonprofit to take that on. We do periodically spotlight male dancers and they are eligible to apply for some of the funds we distribute. Some folks don't appreciate that answer, and I am prepared for that because I have considered that circumstance and a few others already just because I have asked myself (and our small team) question 2: how things might be perceived.

9

Why Is Pushing Back So Hard?

Pushing back and speaking up for ourselves and others can feel hard, there is no denying that. I can't speak from a global perspective on the cultural nuances that make it hard, but I can certainly give a bit of insight into American culture and some of the stereotypes that arise out of it that go a long way toward making folks hold their tongues. I also chatted with a behavioral health psychologist to get some insight into some of the ways that trauma might affect our speaking up and what we can do about managing it. I also chatted with the psychologist about the role power dynamics can play in keeping us quiet as well. Beyond the obstacles that I covered in Chapter 8, which are largely within our control, I didn't want to ignore that sometimes what keeps us quiet is cultural or environmental and we may need some support beyond tactics, which is primarily the focus of this book, to overcome those challenges.

American Culture and Trauma

American culture really prioritizes being nice and getting along with folks. From childhood to adulthood, "being nice," "going along to get along," and "culture fit" are drummed into us. Being well-behaved and compliant leads to being well-liked. Merely speaking up can be seen as being aggressive in American culture, especially if you are not White. Plus, if you are a person of a certain gender, with a certain cultural background, or with a certain sexual identity (and possibly some combination of all three), it can be even more complex. What do I mean? Well, let's dig into it:

- Women who speak up are called bitches. At work, at home, out in the world – everywhere. Take a moment and pop into your search bar "women who speak up called bitch" and there are literally hundreds of articles about it written from a variety of angles.
- Marginalized women have the additional layer of being met with racial stereotypes when they speak up and some when they do not. The angry Black woman and the feisty Latina are common tropes, while an Asian woman might be labeled a "dragon lady" for speaking up and considered a "lotus flower" or "model minority" when she is compliant.
- Black folks are often taught to shrink and tolerate poor behavior, bad service, or even mistreatment. Black men are led to believe they are conspicuous or threatening, and Black women are led to believe they are angry, ignorant, and easily provoked.
- Many children are socialized to "not question adults" and to "do as they are told." These behaviors are often reinforced in schools, and sometimes in church, leading to children who grow up learning to not question authority and carry that mindset into their future careers, relationships, and parenting styles.
- In some cultures, the silence is about safety. Black, Brown, and Indigenous American children are additionally urged to be quiet and well-behaved or even pushed into silence by parents who survived historical abuse and violence by being silent.
- Many immigrant identities stay silent and compliant out of fear they will be forced out of the United States, potentially into a gang-infested or deeply impoverished country.
- Closeted members of the LGBTQIA+ communities also tend toward silence and blending in to keep themselves safe. Speaking up has historically put the lives of some members of these communities at risk.
- Folks with accents from other parts of the world or for whom English is not their primary language stay silent for fear of being judged as incompetent.

These are just a snapshot of the many reasons people stay silent that are connected to discomfort and stereotypes about the uniqueness in our identities. I don't want to downplay the role that race plays in this discussion. When I say American culture, what most folks are going to conjure up in their minds is actually White culture. The reality is that America positions whiteness as the standard. White supremacy culture, also known as whiteness, is the perspective that White people, communities, and culture are superior and are seen as "correct" and valued above others. So many of the examples provided in the bullet list just shown are exacerbated when they are applied to anyone who is not White.

It is hard to speak up when living in your very identity has convinced you that silence is best. "When you are not a part of the dominant identity, silence can be the expectation but also a cover. It can be a source of protection because for those who are marginalized silence offers respite. It's like, 'okay, this is a way that I can protect myself in this moment,'" says Dr. Reisha Moxley, behavioral health psychologist, in an interview we conducted for this book.

Dr. Moxley shared some of what she has seen in her practice:

> Similar experiences many of my American-born Black patients have shared about socialization include how young Black men are socialized, especially from parents or grandparents of an older generation. There's this subtle implication that you look down, like if you're passing a White person or a White woman, you kind of look down; you anticipate that maybe they're afraid. So you are indirectly taught to make yourself smaller. It wasn't explicitly taught but it was something Black men pick up in their upbringing as a reaction to family trauma. And the more I learn about the patient's family history, specifically their significant racial trauma, there are always these ways that elders message, without explaining what happened or why, but the shorthand is, "Sit down and shut up. You're already really conspicuous." So these men make themselves smaller. They avert their eyes, they look down, and it's because we and many of us marginalized people are taught silence can actually save your life.

Sometimes familial, personal, or historical trauma keeps folks silent. As a member of the Black community, I have witnessed ways trauma has played out in my life and the lives of folks around me. I recently heard a story from a friend of mine who is a Black man who recently stopped going to his barber because he wasn't sure how to ask him to make corrections without feeling like he was asking for too much or being too pushy. His barber, also a Black man, has never told him or messaged to him that he was unwilling to cut my friend's hair to his liking; in fact, he has landed the perfect haircut for my friend more than once. "I just feel like every time I ask him to make an adjustment, he is thinking to himself that I am too picky and I'll just find someone else who can do it without me asking. I'm already gay, I just don't want to be seen as the super picky Black guy." I asked him why he doesn't see the haircut as a service he is paying for and consider that the barber might appreciate being given direction. He said, "You're right. I just don't like how much of an opportunity my asking him to cut my hair how I wanted feels like I am reinforcing a stereotype." Yikes. Somehow his personal history has led him to believe his identity is a reason for him to endure poor service and not speak up.

Another example is from a woman who shared a story with me about how she manages a White woman who has spoken to her disrespectfully, stormed out of her office while she was mid-sentence, and has emotional outbursts at her. She shared the story with me, asking for my help, and ended her email with, "Overall I have difficulty speaking up, always balancing how I will be viewed and treated afterwards. 'Angry Black Woman' as a title is a real concern in my environment." Historical trauma has led this woman to believe her identity means she has to endure workplace abuse from a subordinate and cannot speak up without putting her job at risk.

You may be wondering how I recommended each of these folks push back in their respective situations. I revisit both of the scenarios in Part III when I cover what to say in specific kinds of situations.

It is also important to note that although trauma can make it hard for people to speak up, not all trauma results in post-traumatic stress disorder (PTSD). Some folks can have traumatic experiences and be perfectly fine, but if you think it is possible that you are dealing with some personal or familial trauma connected to your identity and it is holding you back from speaking up for yourself, Dr. Moxley recommends "getting some kind of treatment, insight oriented or a trauma processing therapy to deal with the traumatic response or the PTSD. Even if trauma hasn't reached the level of PTSD, insight-oriented work about what experiences you have metabolized as traumatic in your past, and how you have you displayed self-resiliency and moving past traumatic experiences can be useful. What do you do when you run into a similar obstacle? Are you playing a similar narrative or addressing it differently?"

Trauma around identity can also cause some folks to work overtime to conform. This can show up as code-switching, which is adjusting aspects of your identity like your hair, style of dress, or speech patterns in certain situations, particularly in predominantly White workspaces, to align with the perceived norm. Some folks working overtime to fit in are also looking to protect themselves from judgment or scrutiny around their identities, but quite often they long to share more of who they are but don't perceive the space will be made for them to do so. The tricky thing about this thinking is that if no one knows you are hiding aspects of your identity, no one can make room for them. It was this realization for me that made me shift away from relaxing my hair many years ago and why today I can be seen wearing a variety of looks. I want room to be made for me and I want the same for others, so I have to show myself to get there. Otherwise I become the person who says they want change but is working hard to keep things the same. The decision to wear my natural hair is about pushing back on the idea that space cannot be made for me unless I am code-switching or trying to assimilate.

I thought it was important to talk to a behavioral health psychologist for this portion of the book because while I have the lived experiences of trauma and have gotten mental health support to work through it, I am not trained to help others work through it. What I do know is that identity matters are complex and are often cited in studies in which people report reasons they self-harm or have ended their own lives. I am assertive in this book, and I recommend ways that you can assert yourself, but I want to state explicitly that if you need some support with managing trauma, please seek the services of a mental health professional.

Power Dynamics

Power dynamics can also make it hard to push back and speak up. Perceiving that someone has some power over us can make us silent because we don't want to deal with any adverse impact from speaking up. Power dynamics are all around us and also go on our whole lives.

A few common power dynamics that can impede our ability to push back and challenge are:

- Parent/child power dynamics. Many children are socialized to be quiet and to follow parents' rules and, in some extreme cases of abuse, speaking up can have dangerous consequences.
- Employee/employer relationships have power dynamics that can make employees decide it just isn't worth it to push back or speak up because of the potential impact to the employees' livelihood.
- Societal power dynamics that govern how people interact with law enforcement officials and who has access to basics like housing, healthcare, and education.
- Favorability power dynamics that grant exceptions and access to folks who are hard-working, well-liked, tenured, and/or highly influential while providing little to no benefit or cover to those who are also hardworking, but little known, less tenured, junior in their career, and/or less connected.

There is no denying power or the impact to those who have it, but we can all do a better job of having awareness of power dynamics. It is relatively easy to know when you are subject to being in harm's way because someone wields power over you. You sense it. You may try to appease the person, avoid doing things that could make them penalize you, or just try to avoid them altogether. If you are in an oppressive power dynamic, you might not be willing to push back or speak up because of the associated risk. I trust that everyone reading this book is able to evaluate their specific situation to determine if the power dynamic makes room for speaking up. It's also important to know, though, that power is not absolute. Just because someone does have power over you does not make you powerless – all power does not reside with one person. At times we have just gotten accustomed to tolerating the folks with power, rather than pushing back and trying to create some space or balance. Consider the possibility that there might still be an opportunity for you to leverage some of the skills we cover later in this part of the book, paired with some of the techniques in Part III to speak up and push back. In my conversation with Dr. Moxley, she reminded me, "Power is not absolute. There are sometimes subversive and nonsubversive ways that you can empower yourself in a situation or a dynamic where you are not the one in power. Some people use curiosity. I find that I use humor and sometimes folks use vulnerability. There are ways to use all of these to your advantage even when you are not the person who holds most of the power." In the next chapter, I cover tone and approach, where I share some tactics specifically around curiosity and vulnerability.

You may be wondering what you can or should do if you are the person with the power or even how to check yourself to ensure you are not mistreating others with your power. Dr. Moxley shared, "the first thing folks with power can do is be honest with themselves about holding the power." Sometimes folks with power want to be accepted as just a part of the team or relationship without realizing that the fact they hold the power and everyone knows it does impact the dynamic. It is imperative to be honest about having the power. The second step is to ask yourself, how you are using your power. Dr. Moxley says, "Those in power should be thoughtful about the ways that can impact other people with their power. People struggle with that at times because when they really are confronted with the ways in which in the past they've abused or misused their power to perpetuate oppressive systems, often without knowing it, it can feel bad. In many folks coming to these realizations, their immediate response is typically to shut down and then to go into some denial or mitigating, which does not help you to shift your behavior." She continues, "If you want to be responsible with your power, you must quickly move past the denial and mitigating and have a willingness to be in pain and not try to project or avoid the pain associated with your awareness. You must be willing to pay attention to your role in the power differential." In short, it might hurt, but push past that so you can get to a resolution. After that, Dr. Moxley suggests employing some tactics to build trust, which may look different depending on the relationships, but a good place to start is always being willing to take feedback (which we cover in Part I), work to treat people equitably (also covered in Part I), and be consistent.

10 Critical Communication Tools

In this chapter we get into some communication tools I use to help folks we are interacting with to be more amenable to push back regardless of the power differential, the obstacle, and even the circumstances. As I have stated elsewhere in this book, there is always a way to say something and a way for it to land. How we say it is a big part of that. From the language we choose to use to our body language to our tone, mastering a few basics can help you to more confidently challenge or speak up. Speaking of confidence, next I cover some ways to find and use your confidence to help affect your messaging.

Word Choice and Approach

Word choice, approach, body language, and tone are all foundational parts of communicating, but from what I have observed, we don't always employ these elements in the ways that can get the best results for us when we are communicating. When we are considering making an impact, through pushing back or even just sharing a message, we should be thoughtful about how each of these elements can come to life, because any of them can shape how the person or people you are speaking to will receive and react to the message. Let's start with our actual word choices and our approach.

When you are going to push back on someone, there are a few steps you should take to determine your word choice and approach, before you say anything. I usually go through a series of five questions in my mind. You may be thinking, "Five whole questions?" because that might feel like a lot in the moment. Yes, five questions. It is a habit now, so

I can go through them quickly if I need to, but whether I am responding in the moment or typing an email, I still run through these questions:

1. What do I want my message to feel like to the recipient?
2. What is the environment where the message will be delivered?
3. Who else will be present when I share the message?
4. Is this my leader or someone who can influence my experience?
5. What kind of response am I looking for from the recipient?

Let's break each of these down a little. To bring this to life with an example, let's say that you notice a colleague continues to use the expression "fall on deaf ears" in meetings and communications and you want to let them know that their remark is ableist and could be offensive to someone who is deaf or hard of hearing.

What do I want my message to feel like to the recipient?

Obviously we all have different styles and vocabularies so very often these will be personal choices, but as you are deciding what words you are going to use, think about the response you want from the other person. Do you want them to be frustrated? Do you want them to feel moved to act? Do you want them to feel pressured or intimidated? Your word choice has a part to play in the feeling the recipient of your message has when they get it. Use this power to your benefit. When you have a tough message to deliver, but you want someone to receive it and not be angry, you can start by thinking about how you might want the message delivered to you.

Try to push your ego aside when answering this question for yourself. While we sometimes want to confront something, confrontational language is rarely effective at doing anything but enflaming a situation. You might want the person to feel embarrassed or humbled or belittled because you are frustrated. In reality, though, that's you projecting. What you really want to think about with this question is what you want this person to feel like that will be the most effective going forward, rather than how you can bite their head off and make them feel as embarrassed as you feel frustrated.

What is the environment where the message will be delivered?

Are you in a public place where others can hear you? Are you meeting one on one? Are you sending someone an email? The environment dictates your approach along with your word choice. If you are going to address a comment in a meeting, in real time, in front of others the next time a colleague says it, you will want to be succinct but not confrontational, because you don't want to derail the meeting. You might choose to say something like "Instead of 'fall on deaf ears,' let's just say 'the message may be lost.' I'm concerned the other phrase is ableist." Likely the recipient of the message will pause, take in the message, adjust, and keep going. They may even circle back after and ask you to share more. Notice that your word choice did not say "you are ableist"; instead it references the behavior, which reduced the chances of someone feeling accused or attacked. On the off chance that someone says, "What do you mean, ableist?" you can say, "I don't want to derail the meeting, but the use of 'deaf ears' can be offensive to people who actually are deaf. We can discuss it offline, later." Most will take the social cue to move on and engage further after the meeting.

If you are in a one-on-one setting, you may choose to say something more verbose like, "I notice that you use the expression 'fall on deaf ears' often. Are you aware that phrase might be offensive to some folks?" This gives the person you are speaking to the opportunity to realize that their behavior is not inclusive, in an equitable and a safe space to admit they did not know. Using a question invites the person in, so now you can have a dialogue about it instead of a debate or an argument.

Who else will be present when I share the message?

Will you be in a meeting with all senior leaders? Will there be people who do not necessarily know the character of the person you will be addressing? Who will be in the space should matter in how a message is constructed, because who someone is can give us clues to how they might receive a message. If you are delivering a message in front of folks, we want to make sure we are not embarrassing people, because embarrassment is not an effective tool for behavior change. Sure, the person may stop, but embarrassment can make people withdraw altogether or even retaliate. Using the same situation as earlier, if your message is being delivered in front of people who are more senior to you or who the recipient might feel embarrassed in front of, the word choice might evolve some. Still choosing to be succinct, you might say, "In my experience, 'fall on deaf ears' can be offensive to people who are deaf. Can we use another term instead?" This approach invites the folks in the room to join you, which still allows them to stay in their perceived senior position to your subordinate one. Instead of directing, you are inviting.

You might also notice I took out the word *ableist* in this scenario. The larger the room, the more likely someone is not going to know what some terminology means. With larger groups I err on the side of simplifying the message to ensure that everyone has access to the message. In smaller rooms it either is easier to ascertain who is likely to know what a term means or it does not feel like a really big deal if you end up having to explain it.

Is this my leader or someone who can influence my experience?

When it is our leader or someone who can influence our experience, depending on the relationship we have, we are running some risk with addressing their noninclusive or inequitable behaviors. That deserves some attention. If it is your leader and you are in front of people, your word choice using our same scenario might adjust a little more. Perhaps you might instead ask to be invited to the discussion, but in a way where folks are definitely going to give you the floor to speak. That could sound like, "It's a little off topic now, but I heard something a moment ago that caused me some concern. Do you mind if I share?" Once they say "Sure!" – because they will – you can say, "I've heard someone use the expression 'fall on deaf ears' a few times and I am aware that that phrase can be offensive to the disability community. Can we choose another way to say that in the future?" This approach takes the additional step of asking to be invited to the conversation before sharing your concern. In the world of power dynamics, this language lets your leader still feel like the senior person in the room, not be embarrassed in front of their peers or yours, and still be able to receive the message.

What kind of response am I looking for from the recipient?

Contemplating how you want the recipient to respond to you can help you decide the right words to use as well. Going back again to our situation with the ableist phrase, what you most likely want as a response is that the recipient will work on changing their language going forward. Choose words that can enroll your message recipient in the idea that they should shift their behavior. Usually that entails your word choice offering some explanation for why the person should change. Let's review the options we developed for our previous questions:

"Instead of 'fall on deaf ears,' let's just say the message may be lost. I'm concerned the other term is ableist."

"I notice that you use the expression 'fall on deaf ears' often. Are you aware that phrase might be offensive to some folks?"

"In my experience, 'fall on deaf ears' can be offensive to people who are deaf. Can we use another term instead?"

"I've heard someone use the expression 'fall on deaf ears' a few times and I am aware that that phrase can be offensive to the disability community. Can we choose another way to say that in the future?"

You'll note that each of these makes sure to tell the recipient that the messaging, not the person speaking, is offensive. Most folks do not want to be offensive, so they will usually subscribe to changing their behavior. If they actually say they will change during the conversation, that's even better. So the scripts above that ask, "Can we say this differently?" are great for creating an opportunity for someone to say, "Yes, I can do that differently." If folks say yes but then they say it again, you can then hold them accountable using some accountability questions as we discussed in Chapter 8, Overcoming the Most Common Obstacles.

If you get to this last question and you can't come up with what kind of response you want, it is possible that there is nothing for you to say or do at all. When I have gone through the questions and arrived at what I want only to discover I don't want anything or I do not care what the person does going forward, I don't even bother to speak up. It is important for me to be bought all the way in to what I am going to speak up about, which means I have to have a desired outcome.

Just a side note, you can plan what you will say ahead of time in the scenario we are using because you are addressing a behavior the colleague is repeating. This way you can plan to have your script ready when it happens again. I address things in real time because I am practiced – I speak up routinely. If you are new to pushing back, you might not feel like you can address things in the moment just yet. That is okay; keep practicing, and in due time it will be a part of who you are. In the interim, if something happens in the moment that you think needs to be addressed immediately, once you have collected your thoughts, you can chime in and say, "I'd like to circle back to a remark that was made earlier. My apologies for going back, but I have a concern." Needing to circle back usually captures everyone's attention, especially when you share that it is because of a concern. Yes, responding in real time is a useful skill, but get comfortable speaking up first and you will eventually get there.

Practice using the five-question technique for yourself using the following scenario:

> A member of your broader team is named Nonzwakazi (phonetic: Non-zwah-kah-zee). You notice several colleagues tend to mispronounce or shorten her name, and she always corrects them, which you appreciate. However, when she is not in the meeting, people continue to mispronounce or shorten her name and have even called her name "difficult." You want to correct the team, mostly made up of your peers, on how to say Nonzwakazi's name correctly and ensure that they understand name pronunciation is an important part of identity.

Write a few scripts you could use for this scenario using the formula we covered earlier in this chapter.

Body Language and Tone

Lots of us know that body language and tone are important to conversations, but we don't necessarily use them to our advantage. A very popular, and often incorrectly interpreted, study by Albert Mehrabian and colleagues in 1967 found that 93 percent of the emotional impact of a message comes from nonverbal elements.[1] If we are purposeful with our body language and tone, based on Mehrabian's research, we have the ability to heavily influence the emotional impact of a message. If we are honest with ourselves, when it comes to communicating, the mess is in the feelings: how you feel saying it, how you think someone else hears it, how others might hear it. So I'd say having a way to regulate the emotional impact of a message is a pretty big deal.

We really do communicate with our entire bodies, hands, eyes, facial expressions, arms, and how we lean or position our bodies. It is all

---

[1] A. Mehrabian and S. R. Ferris, "Inference of Attitudes from Nonverbal Communication in Two Channels," *Journal of Consulting Psychology* 31, no. 3 (1967): 248–252.

messaging all the time. In facilitating, even virtually, I make sure to use my body to communicate by smizing (smiling with your eyes), keeping my arms open, talking with my hands, and using my smiles. I also speak in an inviting and upbeat tone. I laugh and fluctuate my tone of voice for emphasis. To illustrate how important body language is to inclusive communication, at one point I adjust my facilitation style to a monotone voice, fold my arms, and flatten my facial expression. I look about abstractly as I am speaking. After about a minute of this, I say, "Can you imagine if I had delivered this entire session that way?" Someone always says something like, "I'm so glad you didn't!" Body language and tone change the whole way we experience one another. Let's discuss some ways your body language and tone can help you when speaking up or pushing back.

Let's go back to our scenario from earlier in the chapter:

You notice a colleague continues to use the expression "fall on deaf ears" in meetings and communications and you want to let them know that their remark is ableist and could be offensive to someone who is deaf or hard of hearing.

I'd imagine if you are speaking up about this, you feel frustrated or annoyed about it. We wrote some scripts for how to push back in this situation, right? Let's examine how we can use body language and tone to communicate our message to the recipient. Now, even if we are frustrated and annoyed, we know that those emotions are not ideal to communicate. What most of us do is either say nothing, or if we do say something, we say it as stoically and flatly as we possibly can. After all, this is the workplace – I am communicating information, and lots of folks think that means leave the feels off the table.

Toss that thinking aside.

Remember: 93 percent of the emotional impact of a message comes from nonverbal elements. When people feel, they respond. That is why the first question in the list earlier in the chapter is "How do I want this person to feel?" We like to pretend we leave our feelings at home; we don't. We didn't specify earlier, but let's say we want the recipient to feel accountable for changing their behavior. Let's also say it is our leader we are speaking to, so we are going to use the wording and approach we created from the fourth question we asked: Is this my leader or someone who can influence my experience?

"It's a little off topic now, but heard something a moment ago that caused me some concern. Do you mind if I share?" Once they say "Sure!" you say, "I've heard someone use the expression 'fall on deaf ears' a few times and I am aware that phrase can be offensive to the disability community. Can we choose another way to say that in the future?"

Say this part in your business tone of voice: "Can we choose another way to say that in the future?" You hear that? It's probably a little direct, maybe even cold. Professional, but not really inviting. There may even be a tinge of annoyance in there. That message might rub someone the wrong way.

If I want my leader to feel accountable for changing their behavior, I would use my curious tone and body language for the question. I would say it in the same kind of tone I might say to a good friend, "Do you have plans tonight? I would really love to go out to dinner this evening if you have time." I'd use the same warmth, the same emphasis in my speech pattern, I'd even cock my head a little to the side as I finished speaking. The reason I use curiosity is because people feel inclined to rise to the occasion and address it. When I really want an answer, I turn it on. Think about the tone of voice you use when a child in your life brings you a new toy or book you haven't seen before. Say this next sentence in that tone: "Where did you get this book?" That is curiosity, turned up. Now, say this with that same curious energy: "Can we choose another way to say that in the future?"

Match your body language to your tone. As I mentioned, for curiosity, I often lean my head to the side or I furrow my brow a bit. I want an answer, so if I am in person, I make sure that my arms or hands are not crossed. This way my body language comes across as open, as if I am ready to receive a response, rather than, say, holding my hands in front of me with my fingers interlaced, which can message skepticism.

In later sections in this book I encourage you to use your curious tone or curious energy. The tone I described in the previous exercise and the body language you pair with your version of curiosity is what I mean when I say this. Curiosity works for a great number of conversations that could otherwise seem too abrasive or confrontational; practice it. It might feel exaggerated, but to the recipient, it helps land your message.

The same way you can use your curious energy, you can use humor and vulnerability. I described curiosity first because almost everyone understands curiosity, and almost no one is offended by it unless someone is being too nosy. Humor can mean a wide variety of things to people because everyone has a different sense of humor. Vulnerability is a lot harder to teach because it requires revealing oneself in a relatively private way, which for some folks is completely off the table except with friends and family. But I can share a few tips to help you use either humor or vulnerability in the event you are comfortable doing so.

The main thing with humor is not to be cheesy and artificial about it. If you want to practice using humor, the kinds of situations that it works well for are similar to those curiosity works well for – for example, getting a challenging topic to the table for discussion or holding someone to account. Humor, like curiosity, can invite people to want to respond to you– as long as folks don't feel like you are making fun of them. It helps if you know already that you have a good sense of humor and that your brand of humor works for encouraging discussions.

With humor, make sure if you are going to poke fun at something that the joke or remark isn't offensive. It can be sarcastic or playful, but being offensive defeats the purpose. Humor can be as simple as inviting everyone to laugh along with you on a topic that needs to be discussed. I was in a meeting once where we were designing buttons for a National Coming Out Day event for a client, and one of the buttons had a part you could press that flashed and the button played a short clip of the song "I'm Coming Out" by Diana Ross. It was so, so corny. Playful, but corny. After the song stopped, everyone was kind of quiet for a moment before one of the folks in the room said, "Okay, well, it is certainly fitting for the occasion," and everyone burst out laughing. It was one of those moments where everyone knew the button wasn't the right one for the event, but no one was really sure what to say about it. What made it funny was the timing, and it opened the opportunity for us to get really explicit about what folks wanted the event to feel like – because no one wanted it to feel like that singing button!

Sometimes humor means pushing back playfully on someone. Once, at a former employer, a member of my team, a Black woman, came in with a new haircut. When she walked in, one of the White men on the team said, "Look! She's got new hair!" Without missing a beat she responded with a smile and a playful tone, "And you still have no hair – are we seriously not used to me changing my hair at this point? It's been too long; you're going to make me report you to HR." The White colleague laughed a little, as did the whole room – but he totally got the underlying message. After the laughter he said, "You're right. Thanks for being a good sport, but I shouldn't play like that." As she took her seat she said, "I'm glad you know," and that was that. This situation could easily have turned sour if there were not already established relationships in the room, so be aware of your connections with others before leaning in to using humor.

Vulnerability is super personal and unique to each individual. If you want to use your vulnerability to hold folks responsible or as a means of speaking up, the most important thing you need to know is that folks will get emotional. People might cry, want to connect with you after, and generally express emotion very openly. Heck, you might even cry.

Not long ago I gave a talk about identity for a client that was centered on getting folks to realize you have to be willing to speak up about your own identity so folks can actually include you. I was having a bad hair day and decided to give the talk with a stylish headscarf on. I knew a talk about identity and me wearing a headscarf was a prime opportunity for me to be vulnerable about something I have been facing for over 20 years. As I was wrapping up my talk, after covering all the key points, I decided to lean into my vulnerability. Here is what I said:

> In order for me to hold each and every person that encounters me accountable for respecting the fullness of my identity, I have to be willing to share my identity. It is not easy. Some parts of us are easy to share and others are harder. It's not easy for me to show up with a headscarf on my head. It's not easy for me to show up and tell folks, "Listen, I've been losing my hair for the last 20 years. And soon, I might not have any. It's not easy for me to consider that people may see me one day and go, "Oh my gosh, she's bald. Like, is she sick? Is something wrong?" I wonder all the time what that conversation is going to look like. But how am I ever going to get folks to make room for me – if I won't tell you about me, or if I am offended or defensive, but won't so much as tell anyone why? So I want you to understand that you have to share you; for you, it might be pronouns. It might be your gender. It might be your race. It might be that you prefer differently-abled over disabled or person with disability. It might be not describing you as blind, and instead saying not sighted. It can be anything. If you won't share it, how can we make the room for you that you so crave?

By the end, I was in tears. Thank goodness I can still teach in tears! It was virtual, so folks were in the chat box sending all kinds of love. The funny thing is, I am not super sensitive about losing my hair – it's been a slow process for the past 20 years, I'm sort of ready for when the hair is gone. However, when you use vulnerability to teach, to speak up, to push back – the emotions can come bubbling over, and that's what happened to me in that meeting.

The second thing to know about vulnerability is that you are sharing a part of yourself and that invites people to feel like they can engage with you about it. From that talk, I received so many messages about hair loss, about how to get a hair transplant, about products I could try, about folks who were struggling with the same thing. If I didn't want to talk about my hair, I should not have been vulnerable about it. So if you are going to use your vulnerability to speak up, then make sure you are prepared for what folks will know about you and how they will maneuver with that information.

Whichever tactic you are using – and curiosity, humor, and vulnerability are not the only tools you can leverage – make the body language and tone clear. I often refer to the way adults tend to speak to small children. We emphasize our emotions a little, we speak in kind tones, we use our facial expressions, we speak slowly and use simple language, and we change our tone of voice to get messages across. For example, when I am teaching virtually and I get a troll in the chat box asking rude or silly questions, I don't get mad or offended; instead I want them to stop, so I message disappointment in the way I speak up about it. That often sounds like, "Aww, I'm disappointed you didn't appreciate the video, that's unfortunate. I can't derail the class, though, so if you want to dig in a little more, find me online and we can connect after." I make sure to turn up my disappointed tone of voice and body language. Sort of the same tone I use when my godson, who is four, hits his two-year-old brother: "Oh, don't hit your brother like that. You don't want him to hit you, right?" The tone and energy of that sentence is the tone I use to message disappointment.

You do not have to be cartoonish or silly, but it is worth leveraging the tools we have when it comes to pushing back so we are more likely to get the kinds of responses that help us to move forward. Your language, your approach, your body language, and your tone are tools. Practice using them and you may be surprised at how much you can influence the kinds of responses you want.

Finding Your Confidence

I am asked often where I got my confidence or some variation of that sentiment. It makes me laugh because I don't really feel confident that often. I have rolled this question around in my mind and I even have asked a few friends and a couple of therapists. The most consistent answer I have uncovered is that confidence comes from displaying resilience – which is what I do. While there isn't just one source of confidence, where it comes from is being tested in some way and finding out that when push comes to shove, you can and will push yourself through whatever the challenge is. It is through doing that over and over again that one develops confidence. Confidence is not cultivated in the quiet, it's cultivated in the noise. It's in the experience and the exposures that we have in our day-to-day lives. Pushing through the trauma is part of what helps cultivate the resilience that leads to building confidence.

Largely, the message is that confidence comes from facing the things that feel challenging to you, overcoming them, and doing that continuously. If you are looking for confidence, it's likely not tucked in a book or wrapped up in a message from a dear friend. Confidence is in you, and it is through your own effort that you can discover it. My friend Todd always says, "Things that we think are hard are never as hard as before we begin them. Once you get started and commit, nothing is ever as bad as we think it is."

Burnout and Fatigue

We have talked about trauma and building confidence, so it seems like it would also be important to cover burnout and fatigue. Both of these can arise when you are navigating learning, speaking up, or having discussions about inclusion and equity. Particularly after the murder of George Floyd, when conversations about racial equity and ultimately equity as a whole were amplified, a great many folks were exhausted for several reasons. While I don't think there is a way to avoid burnout or fatigue, there are some perspectives and some tactics I use to manage it.

If the source of your burnout is that you are a member of a marginalized group and are finding that the equity and inclusion conversation is exhausting because it is so personal, let me first say – I feel you. The journey to being seen is a challenging one. After George Floyd's murder, many of my Black friends were like, "I just really want the White folks at my job to leave me alone about being my ally. It is too much to constantly be teaching someone how to support you." I have also heard from several of my nonbinary friends who are exhausted with the folks around them wanting to both know all about pronouns and also failing at using them, leaving my friends to continuously correct. When you are creeping up on burnout, I recommend a few things I do for myself that may help you to manage it:

- Sandwich your day – Start your day with a practice that feels good to you and end your day with a practice that feels good to you. If you like a meditative moment over tea, make time for it at the start of your morning. If you love a good long bath, plan to take one at the end of your day. Your practice might be a quality glass of red wine or a restorative yoga session. Start and end your day with what you know recharges and revitalizes you. Make it a habit so you always know your day will start well and end well.
- Remember the long goal – I find it helpful to remember when I really wished that White people were willing to try to understand that everyone doesn't experience the world the way they do. I remember wanting to teach courses at corporations where I could talk about racial equity and I could cover privilege with the level of candor it deserves. So, while I do feel overwhelmed with the number of people suddenly interested in being allies, and even at times am skeptical of whether it is genuine (pro tip, it doesn't matter), I always remind myself that the comfort I found with the old way was not conducive to the kind of changes I think marginalized identities deserve.
- Ask for accountability – If you are tired of teaching those around you, take some time off from it. It is okay to say to someone, "I have shared my pronouns with you a few times, but I notice I still correct you on it regularly. I'd like to know how I can hold you accountable in a way that requires less labor for me?" Or, "I know you are working hard to be an ally and I appreciate it, but I'm a little overwhelmed with asks right now. What would be helpful for me is if you would be receptive when I ask for help and willing to also give me the option to decline your help at

times. Can we work toward that?" Holding folks accountable can feel tough, but being tough in the moment can help you manage burnout over the long haul.

If the source of your burnout is due to feeling like you are learning and in discussions about inclusion- and equity-related topics regularly, but you are not sure if you are progressing in your learning journey or you are tired of feeling like you are getting it wrong, I have a few tips for you, too:

- Sandwich your day – This is the same advice as previously. Starting and ending your day with something that feels good to you is a great way to beat back burnout for anyone.
- Remember the historical – A lot of people have been feeling unseen and oppressed for a long, long time. While your feelings of being burned out and tired are valid, keep in mind that there are folks whose whole lives have been wrapped up in these matters. Take time to recharge and be careful where you vent about being overwhelmed. Venting to the someone in a marginalized group could feel like you complaining about your privilege.
- Identify some go-to techniques – Learning in the inclusion and equity space can be particularly emotional because it is super easy to take things personally. Everyone has some aspect of identity that is deeply connected to who they are as a person, and that makes having conversations that are necessary also very tough. Establish some techniques that you can go to when you are in conversations that feel difficult for you. It might be asking the question "How would I respond to this if my favorite person said it/did it?" and responding from there. It might be being prepared to ask, "Say more about that?" when you are curious about something that sounds like it might not have been quite right. Having a few tactics handy in the moment can keep you from being worn out when you encounter new situations.

Whatever the source of your burnout, there are a few other things I think that are helpful to keep in mind. First, everyone is tired. At the time of this writing, we are still in a pandemic, in constant debate about vaccine mandates and what the new workplace will look like, managing the global economic fallout from the pandemic impacting shipping logistics, as well as a war as a result of Russia invading Ukraine. Everyone is tired. Try your best to grant some grace to everyone.

I know that is tough. Try to remember, we don't break glass ceilings, or overcome oppression or build inclusive cultures, without some scars. Purposefully plan ways to recharge: vacations, social media or media breaks, spa days – whatever works for you! Many of us are in positions where we do not get the same ample grace we give to others in most spaces and situations while simultaneously trying to be the voice of reason. It is bound to wear you out; plan some downtime.

Finally, if you are the person the racial equity work in your company falls on, sometimes you are burned out because you have to both hold people accountable for showing up in the inclusion and equity space as well as being bound by the social and cultural norms of the workplace. This can lead to people expecting you to hold them accountable for doing the work but also being annoyed with you for holding them accountable for doing the work. The only way you will be able to manage is to have allies who also are committed to doing the work with you. You can't be the only one pushing inclusion and equity forward or you will always be burned out. Get some allies around you and help them see exactly what position your role puts you in and how they have to also see their roles as not allowing you to be the scapegoat that your role could make you.

11 Performative Allyship and Advocacy

Performative allyship and advocacy is when someone with power and privilege professes support and solidarity with a marginalized group publicly in a way that either isn't helpful, is not backed up with meaningful actions, or that actively harms that group. An indicator of allyship or advocacy being performative is that there is some sort of "reward" involved. The reward might be accolades, public acceptance, some degree of favorable visibility, or likes on social media.

A few questions you can ask yourself to assess if a behavior might be performative are:

- What impact will my action have? If you cannot identify an impact, there is a chance there is not one.
- Is my action about me feeling good or being seen as good? If it is, it is likely performative.
- Do my actions benefit someone other than myself or my organization? True allyship and advocacy benefit someone other than you or your company.
- Is a recording involved? Does it have to be? If you are thinking about how best to share it on social and it is inclusion or equity related, it's probably performative.

It's not just people who are performative; organizations can be performative, too. But remember, who makes up organizations? People. If there is ever any doubt that people shifting their behaviors can make a change, remember that the people are the reason it is an organization. This is a big part of the reason that in my work I focus so much on individual behaviors. If enough people change, the whole culture of an organization can change. Let's discuss some of the ways that performative allyship can show up in organizations.

How Organizations Can Be Performative

These days it seems every company is on a mission to add inclusivity to its culture and list of stated values. Truthfully, I love that so many folks have taken an interest! However, the reality is that while there are a good number of companies who want to do the work of building an inclusive and equitable culture, there are still a great many organizations that are only talking about the work of inclusion because the topic is on-trend. There are others that are wholly unsure of how to begin inclusion and equity work at all. Both of these scenarios can result in some challenging workplaces. In fact, it's important to note that organizations can be performative too. Some companies end up doing more harm by not realizing the impact on their staff when they act and speak inconsistently or they are focused on appearing good instead of actually making change.

So, they assign inclusion as a project to someone they have identified as "diverse." Neither tactic is ideal, and neither is going to make a positive impact on a company's culture. In fact, you can end up doing more harm by acting and speaking inconsistently or overburdening someone with an inclusion project they are not prepared to manage.

In the past few years, there has been a trend in organizations where the more senior Black, Indigenous, Hispanic, or Latinx/Latiné/Latina/ Latino person – very often a woman – gets asked or forcefully volunteered to take on managing the organization's diversity and inclusion efforts. The ask to take on this work is often framed as an invitation to "play an important role in the company" and have an "impact on the entire organization." Rarely is the ask accompanied with an offer of additional human capital to support the work or a substantive budget, but the standards for producing results are usually high.

If you are a leader in an organization who has made or is considering making the kind of request I just described, perhaps innocently or even well-intended: stop. It isn't the right approach. I imagine you may be thinking that the most adjacent senior leader who is not White could be a good fit to lead inclusion work since race and ethnicity are big parts of the work of inclusion. Let's talk about why this approach is not ideal:

1. Very often the recipient of the ask to take on a company's diversity and inclusion work feels compelled to say they will it take on, even if they do not want to or feel they do not have the capacity to do so. Essentially, you may be unintentionally burdening your talent and not setting them up for success – and because if the person you have asked is underrepresented on the team or in the organization, they may not have the psychological safety to decline the additional work without fearing retaliation. It is also possible that they are secretly working double-time already to demonstrate they belong on a team where they are underrepresented.

2. Inclusion and equity work is a business imperative: business imperatives should not be added to busy leaders' plates as ad hoc projects, but instead be assigned human capital and budgets. How serious are you about your organization's inclusion and equity objectives? Your investment should reflect that commitment.

3. Inclusion and equity work requires expertise. Expertise is not just the lived experience of being a Black person or a woman or from another country (or whatever uniqueness someone has as a part of their identity). Yes, there are folks who will lead you to believe that their personal experience is all it takes to be able to lead the work, but that is completely untrue. While personal experiences can contribute to someone's passion, they do not mean much for their expertise. If you or your company is committed to making an impact on inclusion, expect to hire talent or consultants with both expertise and experience to help you deliver.

Ultimately, assigning inclusion and equity work as a project is performative allyship. It is saying you care about making a difference and an impact, but you are not actually taking meaningful action on making it happen. Supporting the work of inclusion and equity for an organization requires the same kind of strategy, commitment, and investment that other business objectives require.

Some of you reading are or have been on the receiving end of an ask to take on leading the inclusion and equity work for your company. Maybe you are a new executive or perhaps you are vocal about your company being purposeful about inclusion and leaders have sensed your passion. The next thing you know you have been "voluntold" to lead diversity, equity, and inclusion for your team, division, or company. Maybe you aren't sure you know what to do and, more importantly, you aren't sure you have the bandwidth to take on anything additional. Good news; you don't have to take on any additional work and there is a way to say no. I explore how to react to this type of ask in depth in Chapter 16, Saying No While Still Protecting Your Reputation. Feel free to skip ahead and read that section if you are looking for support today.

There are a few other common ways I see organizations show up performatively:

- "We want to hire more diverse talent, but the talent isn't there." This is almost never true. There are some companies that are not really making efforts and are paying lip service. There are also occasions where companies really need to hire some consultative support to help them think differently about where to find talent or, more importantly, how to create inclusive access and inclusive job descriptions.
- "We'd like more board/executive team diversity, but we haven't found anyone qualified." Again, the talent exists. The reality is that board and executive leadership team opportunities mostly arise out of people's networks and most folks do not have diverse networks. If folks want diverse boards they have to change their approach to how board and executive role seats are filled or they have to diversify their networks. The current processes are not working.
- "We are having a hard time finding vendors and partners who are diverse." This is another case of needing to change the strategy being used to find folks. Most large companies that use vendors and partners can absolutely diversify, and in fact the government incentivizes it.
- "We would like to diversify our corporate giving and community investment dollars." Folks don't always like to hear this, but money talks. Inclusion costs dollars and requires investment of resources just like any other business strategy. How much folks are willing to invest can say a lot. Also, donations to organizations in need should be more than your top-tier historically Black colleges and universities (HBCU) or your most recognizable non-profits. A company really looking to make an impact is going to go a step further to see who is truly in need, not just who is most visible.

I work with a number of large corporations and in our consulting calls, I am as honest with them as I am here about this list and much more. In many cases, just like my clients, I don't think folks intend to be performative, but in the absence of knowing what to do, people imitate whatever behaviors are on display around them. Which is why we see so many companies making the same exact efforts around inclusion and equity, even when the approaches may not yield the best results. I am sharing these ways performativeness shows up in companies not to embarrass anyone or call anyone out but to highlight some areas of opportunity where impacts can be made and to show just how easy it is to slip into being performative instead of impactful.

Avoiding the Inclusion and Equity Olympics

Another way I have seen performative inclusion, allyship, or advocacy come to life has been in the form of what I refer to as the inclusion and equity Olympics. Snarky, I know, but what does it mean? It refers to someone making a grand or very visible gesture of being an ally, being inclusive, or calling out inequity. This can show up in real spaces or virtual ones, and it usually entails someone who considers themselves an ally overreacting to something and often in a very assertive or rude way that is unwarranted but can garner a lot of attention – kind of like an Olympic sport. Let me share a few examples.

I once supported a client who shared with me that they were rolling out a newsletter that detailed the history of racist words. I found it strange, having worked with the client and knowing their culture wasn't rife with racist language, so I asked, "Are you hearing people using inappropriate words in the office?" The response was, "Oh, not at all, but we think people need to be aware that words like master bedroom, blacklist, and cakewalk have a racist history." I shared, "If no one is using the words, why introduce them into the company culture? A better approach is to look at an issue that is occurring and work toward addressing it instead." The client was so eager to be an ally that they were going to introduce a problem no one even had so they could inform folks about it.

Another example is once when I was facilitating a class where I stated, "We have to remember inclusion also includes those who are disabled" and someone chimed in and said, "Don't use disabled – you should know better. People with disabilities do not like that term!" I said, "I have a couple of people in my life who are very particular about both terms: one prefers disabled and the other wants to be called a person with a disability.[1] Are you a member of the disability community? Is there a word I can use to be inclusive when speaking with you?" The person retorted, "I am not disabled, but I am an ally and you should not say that." I said, "I can appreciate your attempt at allyship at this moment, but is it possible you are misguided? I used both terms to be inclusive and it sounds like you are angry about word use that isn't negatively impacting you or the community you are attempting to be an ally for. How is your approach in this meeting role-modeling allyship?" The person stopped speaking. There was no violation or offense warranting such a visceral response, but instead, it felt like they saw chiming in as an opportunity to challenge me as the facilitator in front of the group. In fact, prior to that exchange, they interrupted several other times. Their objective wasn't allyship, but instead performing for attention.

A final example of behavior that could be classified as inclusion Olympics is when someone chimes in to address someone about something that is not only not problematic, but also not really their business. I have a good friend, a Black man, who calls me "Red," and he has called me that since I was a teenager. My friend and I were in the airport, and I was looking for him because he went to find seating while I went to the restroom. He sees me looking for him and calls out, "Red!" and I head over. As I was making my way to him, a White woman seated near to him says, "Did you call her Red? You shouldn't call her that. It's disrespectful and colorist." My friend totally ignored her. I approached and joined him in the seat next to him. A few minutes later the woman ended up moving seats and my friend told me what happened. While she was sitting near us, the woman didn't say anything else to him or me, but honestly, she shouldn't have said anything to begin with because obviously our interaction was not harmful, nor was it her business to engage. While it is true that "red" and "redbone" as references for light-skinned women are terms that are rooted

---

[1] The term *differently-abled* has fallen out of favor, but there are still folks who would prefer it; some others will say physically challenged or person with a disability. In private spaces, I tend to use only disabled. Similar to *Latinx*, there will be folks who won't appreciate the term and may correct you. In such a case, just receive the correction and adjust.

in colorism, the terms are also community language for members of the Black community. The woman's attempt to address colorism at that moment was misguided and not useful.

I am not suggesting that you give up working to be inclusive and equitable to ensure you are avoiding behaviors one could consider the inclusion or equity Olympics. I'd like you to ensure that when you are speaking up about matters of inclusion or equity, you have at least assessed whether your speaking up is performative or impactful. Are you seeking to protect someone or ensure they have access to some privileges you have, or are you trying to show off your knowledge and "check" someone's behavior because you think you know better? Are you addressing a real problem or a manufactured one? The times when someone (especially rudely) chimes in to correct or address behavior that isn't actually harming or excluding anyone, or works overtime to address behaviors that aren't even happening, are times when the inclusion and equity Olympics may be at play.

Avoiding the Oppression Olympics

There is another term floating around, "oppression Olympics." It refers to one oppressed group of folks going to great pains to show how they are more oppressed than another group – often to get more attention. The oppression Olympics is tricky to discuss because most folks are able to more closely identify with the kinds of oppression that they most likely experience. Since there are no universally agreed-upon measures, oppressed groups can end up competing with one another to highlight who is more oppressed and therefore of more importance. In the months that followed the Black Lives Matter movement protests against police brutality in the summer of 2020, there was a rash of hate crimes committed against Asian folks in the United States, and it gave way to the hashtag #StopAsianHate. Many folks in support of the Black Lives Matter movement felt like the Asian community was asking for solidarity from the Black community for #StopAsianHate but were not vocal when #BlackLivesMatter movement protests were happening. This bred competition between the two underrepresented identity groups about who was more oppressed and therefore who deserved more attention. The oppression Olympics perpetuates division and ultimately does not further the agenda of any oppressed identity; it simply vies for attention, which is why it is in this book under performative allyship.

Every oppression is awful and every oppression is unique. No struggle is so great as to erase any other oppression. If you encounter a circumstance where you are leaning in as an ally for one group and someone attempts to challenge you by saying you should be in support of another because "they are worse off" or "deserve to be the focal point" or any language like that, you can push back by saying something like, "I am not ignoring any struggles or information. I recognize that there are many marginalized identities. I don't put historical discrimination and violence in competition with each other." Alternatively, you can say something like, "Thanks for sharing that. I'd love the opportunity to talk about that with you another time. Right now I am focused on [insert focus] ."

Additionally, you get to decide where you want to lend your attention and your allyship. If the personal cause you are leaning in to is autism, that's fine. You have your reasons why. I tend to support Black trans women and Black activism; I have my reasons why. The key mindset that you want to have is that everyone (who is not doing malice or harm) deserves equity and to be included. It is worth learning the ways different identities have experienced oppression. You may find over the course of your life that you will support a great many causes and be an ally and an advocate for many communities. That doesn't mean you have to be out front on every single issue for every single person. There are some folks who want to try to do that, but it is not required and for many of us, it is not really possible. My approach is to always work to live my life as an inclusive and equitable person. I still get to have my personality, interests, and focal areas, and I do have them. But as a general matter, in all that I do and am, I strive to be inclusive and equitable and am always open to correction.

As I have spent this chapter speaking about how to use all the tools at your disposal when you are messaging, it is important to note that there are a group of folks who are not neurotypical who can still miss a lot of the social queues, body language, tone, and word choice nuance we covered earlier. Remember when I said there are not any absolutes? If you encounter someone who is neurodivergent, it just means that their brain processes information in a way that is not typical. Folks with ADHD or autism are considered neurodivergent. Despite commonly held ideas, you may or may not notice someone is neurodivergent, but if you do, the best thing is to do your best to adapt to a communication style that works best for that individual. There isn't a universal recommendation because every neurodivergent person will be different, but the willingness to adapt is always a good step to take toward inclusion and equity.

12 Pushing Back and Speaking Up – A Pep Talk

In this last chapter of Part II, I want to leave you with some words of encouragement and a bit of perspective to help you speak up and advocate for those around you. I also am a big believer that we need to understand what we should expect for all the labor that we may need to give to something. At this point in this book it is pretty clear that labor is part of speaking up. Whether it is getting out of our own way or figuring out the right words and approach, there is some work involved. So if you are going to put in all that labor, let's cover what some of your expectations should be.

When I am engaging with folks, I look for five main boundaries for me to be willing to engage in the discussion. These are things I can commit to giving to each engagement and I expect them back. They are:

1. **You deserve to be heard** – *Heard* in this context to me means that you should feel welcomed to speak up (even if you are nervous); you should not be met with shutting down or other behavior that indirectly messages that you should be quiet.
2. **You deserve to be respected** – *Respect* in this context means that you are not at risk of physical harm or verbal mistreatment or abuse from being a part of the dialogue.
3. **You deserve to ask questions and get clarity** – Asking clarifying questions is important to any growth conversation where there is an exchange of ideas.
4. **You deserve to have your ideas and contributions respectfully acknowledged** – Having your ideas and contributions acknowledged respectfully means you get credit for the work you have done. This might mean a simple thank you for your

help, being quoted (as I have done with a few folks throughout this book), or even having someone highlight your impact on a project in a meeting with leaders.

5. **You deserve access to information and resources relevant to your survival or success** – You should be able to access help when you need it. With the exception of private or confidential information, when engaging you should be able to get whatever information you need to engage responsibly.

You deserve to have discussions and conversations with others that are fruitful and productive. For me, when one of these boundaries is crossed, it can be an obstacle to the conversation's being effective, and I am likely going to decide to disengage and try another approach – potentially with a different person altogether. What do I mean by a boundary is crossed? I can share a few examples:

- *Being heard*

    If someone does not want to hear me and they message that, I let it go. In a recent training class a woman did not like a video I played. I offered, "I'd love to talk more about it. If you find me on LinkedIn or Instagram I can listen to more of your perspective and share more of mine." She dropped in the chat, "No, I don't want to talk about it; the video is terrible and you will not change my mind." Okay. I will not be heard. No need to press on.
- *Being respected*

    I am willing to have a conversation with just about anyone, but respect is the minimum necessary. I will not tolerate degradation, yelling, putting my safety at risk, embarrassment, or anything else that is disrespectful. We don't have to speak, there is sure to be another alternative that won't require disrespect. I also categorize gossiping under this. If someone is gossiping to me or about me, I disengage.
- *Asking questions*

    If I cannot ask you questions, then how can I make sure we are understanding one another? The same goes for you. A dialogue requires that we have the ability to check understanding. This isn't the same as checking to understand someone's reasons, which we covered earlier. That kind of understanding is not essential. I mean understanding from a comprehension standpoint. If folks are unwilling to answer questions, most times I will completely disengage. For example, when I moved to Maryland I went to the DMV to get my license changed, but the online rules were so confusing I wasn't sure I had everything I needed. I went in and picked a number that was a long way from the number who they were helping. So, I decided to ask the security guard if there was anyone who could tell me if I had what I needed to change my license because I would hate to wait and not have everything. He laughed at me and said, "That number you have is the only way you can get your questions answered." I decided to leave. There had to be a better way, and I learned quickly that there was. After asking questions of some of my Maryland friends, I learned that everything was county driven in Maryland, which made it so much clearer what I needed to do to get my license. Questions are essential to gaining clarity. I also offer some powerful questions that can be used for a variety of occasions later in this part of the book.

Idea and contribution acknowledgment

Idea and contribution acknowledgment lets you know you are valued and supported. If you think back to how we defined inclusion, value and support were important ways to include folks. It does not have to be a big deal, but when someone uses my words, I expect them to attribute them correctly. When I am the source of an idea, a thank you goes a long way. If I sense that someone is taking my ideas and contributions without acknowledging me, it feels like theft or like I am being used. I worked with a woman once where the role we were in was so large two of us were needed to fill it. It made sense and almost required that we collaborate to get the work done. I started to notice that she wanted to get together and ideate, but once the idea was formed (mostly my ideas), she would present it to our leader as if she came up with it and was working with me to get it done. After I realized what was happening, I stopped partnering with her to create ideas. Since we worked together I had to share what I was doing so we could do our job, but I would build my idea out, then present it to her in front of our leader so he could watch how the process truly unfolded instead of risking her not acknowledging my role in the strategy creation.

■ *Access to essential information*

While it is impossible to know everything, my expectation when engaging with anyone is that they will tell me what I need to know, or if I ask for something I need that they have access to, they will share it. Part of inclusion is setting someone up for success. Withholding information or only sharing partial information when it comes to my survival or career is a hard line for me. We all have to navigate so many unknowns; once I realize someone is purposely not providing pertinent information or being strategic about its use, I stop engaging.

All of these boundaries are guides – there is always the chance of an exception. Sometimes someone doesn't realize they aren't acknowledging your contributions, or folks are upset and yelling and we are making room for their emotions. So there are times we may flex, but these boundaries can help you set some expectations around how you should expect to be engaged with. I've said it before: you may be uncomfortable doing the work of equity and inclusion, but you do not have to be degraded, attacked, used, or belittled.

Sometimes folks ask me how I confront random acts of inequity out in the world. The honest answer is, most times I do not. Confrontation with strangers means I am putting myself in a circumstance where the person does not have to hear me, and they may elect not to respect me. Are there times I have done it? Absolutely. But barring situations where someone is in danger and I am able to help, my engagement with strangers on inclusion and equity is a nonstarter.

In fact, remember those questions I shared with about overcoming fear of speaking up in Chapter 8, Overcoming the Most Common Obstacles (under the heading "Fear")? To recap, they were:

1. What happens if I say or do nothing?
2. Is anyone hurt by my silence? If so, who?
3. Does anything change for the better or worse if I speak up?
4. Is my silence worth it?

Before you decide to confront someone out in the world you do not know, consider those four questions. If any of those answers do not pan out, then continue on with your life. Very often the third and fourth questions stop me in my tracks with strangers. "Does anything change for the better or worse if I speak up?" *I don't know. The person might listen, or I could end up in an escalated encounter with someone I don't know that puts me in danger.* "Is my silence worth it?" *My silence is worth my safety, so yes.*

There are so many folks in the world who are interested in learning about and engaging on inclusion and equity; reserve your energy for those folks. Save your pushback and speaking up for spaces that impact you and folks you know. Saviorism will have us thinking it is our job to correct everyone all the time, and that isn't reasonable. It also might isolate you because as I have mentioned elsewhere in this book, the objective is to make inclusion and equity a part of your life, not make them something to do.

The Benefits of Pushing Back and Speaking Up

I think if you are reading this book, you are probably in the frame of mind that speaking up is a skill you could use or want to get better at, but I want to very pointedly offer some of the benefits of speaking up for when you are finding the muscle to do it scared. Some of these have been touched on throughout the text, but just in case you missed them, let's list out the benefits here:

- Speaking up for yourself and others is rewarding because it gives you a chance to make an impactful change. Sometimes that change happens immediately, sometimes it takes time, but the impacts from speaking up are often beneficial long term. Think about the civil rights movement or more recently the #MeToo movement and the generational impacts that have come from those folks speaking up.
- Speaking up helps to shape culture because it sets the expectations and standards for behavior. Allowing poor behaviors to go unchecked reinforces them; speaking up for what is inclusive helps keeps the standards at the forefront. A few short decades ago many things that casually happened in the workplace would not be tolerated now – racial slurs, sexual harassment and abuse, sexist remarks. Just watch an episode of *Mad Men* to get an idea of

how workplaces of the 1950s and 1960s looked. Folks speaking up and advocating is how workplaces and society at large change.

- Speaking up allows us to use our power and privilege to be allies and advocates. It is one of the powerful tools I am always teaching as a way to role-model inclusion as an ally or an advocate.
- Speaking up gives us a chance to pay it forward. As I mentioned above, there are generational changes that have come as a result, which means we have all likely benefited from someone speaking up. Paying it forward is a great way to keep the impact going.
- Speaking up gives you a chance to ensure equitable access and treatment. Sometimes folks don't know what's available, when they are being offensive, where they can improve, and much more. As we discussed we can all benefit from a bit of feedback, and very often speaking up is the means for folks to get the feedback that will cause them to create more equitable access and experiences for folks. An example from my own life is in the past decade or so I became aware of how large companies use their boards, but board service for myself wasn't on my radar until I went to a meeting on board readiness for women that a friend invited me to. He helped put the event together with his company because he believes more women need access to the information that can help them get onto corporate boards.

Just because you can't always see it, speaking up can sometimes surprise us with the impact it can make in the long run. My girlfriend, who also works in the inclusion and equity space, was talking to her daughter about an activity they do in her first-grade classroom, where at one of the learning stations, her teacher colors people. Elle, who is six, almost seven, years old, says, "My teacher always colors the people with a tan crayon." Mom asked, "how did that make you feel?" to which Elle said, "well it makes me not feel seen because all people are not tan, and she always uses tan." Mom later emailed the teacher about the conversation she and Elle had and asked if there was an opportunity to discuss how they were fostering diversity in the classroom.

The teacher responded by saying she appreciated the situation being brought to her attention and felt terrible that Elle felt that way. She agreed to shift her behavior at the coloring station and was open to having some discussion about ways to better foster diversity in the classroom. It didn't stop there, though. Going forward, in the syllabus, instead of just asking for the kids to have a box of crayons, they now ask for the kids to have the Crayola Colors of the World™ skin tone crayons. So speaking up not only changed the class Elle was in but also the experiences for future classes.

There are many more reasons why speaking up has its benefits; some may even be very personal to you. I know I definitely am more inclined to see the value of speaking up when it is a cause or circumstance that resonates with me for personal reasons. Keep the benefits in mind when you find yourself needing that little push to speak up. Remember, if we continue to say nothing, we can't complain or be frustrated when nothing changes for the better.

Language and Tactics

As a general matter, we don't control much. Life arbitrarily throws unexpected curveballs and celebratory moments at us and we are pretty much in a position to adapt and survive. We do get to control a special few things in our lives, and one of those things is how we interact with others. To simplify, I tell my mentees, "You control your own experience." You teach people how to treat you through your own behaviors and you get a say in how your life feels to you. The folks around us pick up on subtle and not-so-subtle queues in your behavior that message your boundaries, your openness, your confidence, and much more. The best advice I can give you is to treat yourself how you want to be treated. That sounds super simple and cliché, but in more cases than not, it is effective if you embody it.

What do I mean by "treat yourself how you want to be treated"? I mean that if punctuality means a lot to you, you should be punctual. If you want folks to be responsible with your time, you should be concise and efficient with others. If you want to have warm and meaningful connections with your colleagues, you should be warm and build relationships. If you show up confidently, respectfully, and come across as being prepared, you will find that people will expect you to be confident (even when you are nervous), they will treat you respectfully, and when someone is unprepared (even if they are the leader), they will apologize for not being prepared.

You also have to speak about yourself how you want to be spoken about. In most cases, especially in a workplace setting, people will react to and follow the model you set. If you speak about being responsible, considerate of others, committed to execution, and a culture champion, people will literally begin saying those things about you to others. Be responsible and thoughtful about what you want others to say about you, because people will repeat it and they will treat you in alignment with it. I remember a stretch of time in my career where I would refer to myself as direct and raw to let folks know I was going to be straight-forward and authentic. It wasn't long before people started to describe me to others as direct and raw in a culture that saw those words as threatening. Yikes. I had to work double-time to course-correct on that messaging so that folks at my company understood that I wasn't threatening, but rather that I was candid and genuine. You basically tell people what to think about you, so make it a narrative that works for you and that you can live up to with integrity.

I must add that you should actually deliver on your messaging. You can sell yourself as a confident and authentic leader, but if you don't deliver, folks figure that out pretty quickly. You've probably had the experience where someone says they can do something and then they underdeliver. The disappointment that you feel when you discover that person isn't who they said they were is the same feeling people have when you don't deliver on the personality, skill, and energy your words have promised. Do the actual labor of truly being the person you want to be treated as: the well-respected leader, the responsible and skilled communicator, the organized culture champion, the confident and candid professional. Remember, through your own behavior, you are teaching those around you how to treat you. You are advocating for how people will treat you by how you role-model your treatment of yourself.

13

A Short Lesson on Boundaries and Staying Focused on the Goal

Don't take the ball when it isn't yours. In other words, if something is not yours to resolve or address, no matter what happens, do not take ownership of it. Take it as a lesson from me; there are people in this world who operate well within their boundaries. Lots of them are not burned out, they do not feel guilty, and they are not carrying unreasonable workloads. Furthermore, they are thriving, getting treated well, and seeing performance appraisals with high ratings.

Don't take on responsibilities that do not belong to you. Even if you can do it easily. Even if you can do it better than the person whose job it is, don't take it on. Even if you are interested in the work, unless you want the work to be your unpaid job, do not take it on. Here's the thing: when you take on things that are not your role and you do them well, they become your role, whether you mean for them to be or not. Sure, occasionally you may take on something as a stretch assignment to help you get promoted – that's fine, as long as you are in communication with your leaders about why you are taking it on and what the expectations are. But in just about every other case, don't take things on or you will find that whoever's job it really is will be the one collecting the paycheck and you will be the one doing the work. This even goes for asking for support from customer service people or solving a workplace issue that is impacting you and the rest of your team – you can make recommendations, you can even share what will solve it – but if you actually do it, you might soon discover that the work is yours and you will be laboring more than you intended.

For example, imagine you used to manage the employee survey at your former company. Your current company comes to you when they decide that they are going to implement an employee survey. You share that it is a good idea and that you are willing to answer any questions they have in the process. You do not say, "I am willing to help wherever you need me." There is a difference. One means "I will share my expertise should you need it." The other messages "I will labor to help this thing happen." Keep your capacity and goals at the forefront; otherwise, you will end up taking on all kinds of labor you do not have bandwidth for in the spirit of being helpful.

Here is an example: I ordered a virtual gift card for a friend's baby shower that I could not attend. When she went to load it to her account with the retailer, some weird error happened, and it did not load. She called customer service to try to get it resolved, and they told her because I purchased it, I needed to call. So I got someone on the line in customer service and said, "Hi, I'm calling because I purchased a virtual gift card. I sent it to someone, but she was not able to load it into her account. She called, and though I cannot see the error on my end, because it says the gift card was delivered, she can't access the gift card. What I would like is for you to either refund the gift card to me or to reissue the gift card to her. One or the other is what I think would be a good solution, unless there's something else that you think would work better."

Their customer service person asked for the details to look up the gift card and said, "Oh, I see it here. It looks like it was delivered." I sat silently. In my brain, I was reminding myself that I knew what the problem was and the customer service rep was still sorting it out. They needed the grace to figure it out, so I could wait in silence. After a few seconds the customer service person said, "Ma'am?"

I replied, "I'm here."

They repeated, "The gift card was delivered. It doesn't appear to have been used."

I said, "Yes. Would you like for me to repeat my concern? It sounds like you might not have followed my request."

"Sure," they said.

"Great. I'm calling because I purchased a virtual gift card. I sent it to someone, but she was not able to load it into her account. She called, and though I cannot see the error on my end, because it says the gift card was delivered, she can't access the gift card. What I would like is for you to either refund the gift card to me or to reissue the gift card to her. One or the other is what I think would be a good solution, unless there's something else that you think would work better."

"I understand," the customer service person said, and added, "Just one moment."

Several seconds later, the customer service person said, "I see the gift card here, it looks like it was delivered, and it looks like it wasn't used yet." I sat there again in silence. I was frustrated, but, again – I knew the person helping me was new to this situation and was trying to get up to speed. My frustration wasn't useful to either inform or to chastise, so I waited. The person again asked if I was there, and I again confirmed that I was, and they repeated the same thing yet again.

I finally said, "Can you help me understand how that is a solution to my call? If you aren't following my concern, I recommend you ask me some more questions or find someone who can assist." I was placed on hold again. I was not about to repeat myself a ton of times – it takes so much energy to keep saying the same thing over and over to someone who is clearly not even trying to understand. So I didn't. I am never rude, but I will message clearly, confirm understanding, and then wait for a response. As a general matter, I am not about to get angry; instead, I am going to ask the person whose job it is to solve the problem what to do solve it, and wait for a solution. If it takes too long, I will leave contact information and wait for a call back. Too often I see folks get emotional and escalate, which only makes matters more time consuming because now you not only have the issue you called about, you also have to express the frustration you are currently experiencing while repeating a story. It's too much labor and it detracts from the goal.

With the gift card matter, some time later the person came back on the line and said, "I have refunded the gift card, and I can reissue another one." We went through that process and the gift card issue was resolved. When you lean in and start doing the work for the person who it belongs to, either by giving directives ("Have you tried to refund the card? Why isn't that working?") or taking on more than you can or should ("I am happy to help wherever you need me"), you essentially take on the labor and detract from getting to a resolution. Stop taking on more than you can handle or work that doesn't belong to you. I call this "not taking the ball."

Not picking up the ball and staying firm with boundaries that protect you is also important in your personal life. Many years ago I took on the labor of caring for a sick family member whose daughters were living in various other states. Funny thing is, I also was living in another state. But I stepped in and began flying back and forth to care for my family member. After some time, my life evolved and I was living in one state, working in another, and still traveling to a third to take care of my loved one. I had stepped in because it seemed like no one else would. I was burned out and it was wearing on me financially, but I kept it up. When I finally stepped back, all of her children figured out how to address the situation. You may think the ball will drop without you, but chances are it won't. And if it does, right when it does, someone will step in, ready to clean up the mess. Protecting your energy, boundaries, and time are ways you can role-model advocating inclusion and equity for yourself.

Exercise your boundaries. Your job is your job. If you don't want the work or really can't take it on, don't take it on. If you are unsure how to say no to additional work, I cover that in Chapter 16, Saying No While Still Protecting Your Reputation. If you are worried something won't get done unless you step in, most times it is still worth it not to take it on and to wait and see what happens.

I use the "don't take the ball" technique in a lot of conversations – when folks try to pull me in to work that isn't mine, want to pick my brain, or want to put me in a position to lead when it is not my role. Because these are such useful tactics, I offer another example.

Imagine your leader comes to you with a goal he has discussed before, around "retaining more millennial and Gen Z female talent." Now imagine, you are not in recruiting, so the retention objectives and tactics fall outside your functional skills, but maybe they connect to an aspect of your identity – perhaps you are a woman, or Gen Z. When your leader asks you to take the project on, your response should be something like:

> "I am concerned about retaining more millennial and Gen Z female talent, but my skill set doesn't align with the goal. Can we find a partner to assist who has the proper skill set?"

Let's say the leader pushes by saying something like, "Sure, but I want you to lead it because I think you have the lived experience to know what we are looking for in talent."

Your push back would sound like, "I appreciate your compliment, thank you. I don't believe my lived experience will add up to success in recruiting talent, I think we should find someone who knows recruiting. I am happy to serve as a business resource as that person looks to define their approach to millennial and Gen Z talent, since I do have lived experience. Can we take that approach?"

Imagine your leader might say, "It sounds like you are not interested in a stretch assignment."

Your response is, "I am totally interested in a stretch assignment that aligns with my career goals. I am not sure this project aligns, and more importantly, I think the objective of retaining more millennial and Gen Z female talent is too important to rest in my novice hands. I am grateful that you are so confident in me. Can we discuss other stretch opportunities that might be a better fit?"

Never take things on that do not align with your goals or interests. If the assignment goes wrong, you can be blamed. If it goes well, it can become a part of your role that you are never compensated for. If you are going to take on something as a special project, ensure that you get clarity about expectations and outcomes both for the project itself and for what it will mean for you personally.

Asking Powerful Questions

Powerful questions are questions and statements of curiosity that can work in a myriad of situations if you leverage the right body language and tone. With each of these, lean in to your curious energy as we discussed in Chapter 10, Critical Communication Tools, under the heading "Body Language and Tone." It is also helpful in some cases to turn on your confusion and the body language and tone that you associate with that. Sounding confused when asking a powerful question evokes a response in the listener. When people sense confusion, they tend to want to clear things up, which in some cases is what you want to happen. Here is a short list of some of the powerful questions (and two statements) I use the most.

- Can you say more about that?
- How might that look in action?
- Can you help me see how you arrived at that conclusion?
- Have we/you explored any alternative solutions?
- What's keeping you from believing ____ as a possibility?
- Are you open to hearing another perspective?
- What might we be overlooking?
- Is it possible that there is a better approach?
- Can I have some additional context?

- Hmm, I'm not sure I follow.
- I think I need a bit more information before I can react.

I often precede a powerful question with a guiding expression that sets the tone, like "Oh, wow!" or "Hmm" or "That's interesting" or "Oh, my." For my communication style it helps to let folks know the sentiment I want applied to my messaging because sometimes I can come across as a little too direct. If you are a bit more reserved, you may elect not to use these additional expressions. Fine-tune your approach with powerful questions so it works best for you and your style.

14 Avoid People-Pleasing and Resentment

There are few ways to undermine your own self-respect, confidence, and influence faster than people-pleasing. It is so, so easy to do and in the moment, we can believe that it is a sure path to being liked. In reality, people-pleasing sets you up to be used over and over. Folks can sense that you really want to be liked and you are willing to sacrifice important parts of yourself to get that acceptance. Don't be tempted, not even for senior leaders or new family members – never, ever do things just to be liked. And let me be clear, folks will try to get you to do things just because it will make them happy – folks are going to ask things you would not consider asking yourself. Standing up for yourself requires you to protect your time, your brand, and your credibility by avoiding people-pleasing behaviors.

You may be wondering how you can avoid people-pleasing behaviors at work, especially if the person doing the asking is in a more senior position or you support them or their team as a business partner. The urge to have a relationship where you are well-liked can easily lead you to say yes to things you shouldn't in this kind of situation. Let's explore an example.

One of my coaching clients was assigned to work as a business partner with a very-high-profile leader who was new to the organization. He was junior to her in job level and was accountable for supporting her team with defining how they were going to bring the larger company's inclusion goals to life in her part of the business. After the dust of her being new to the business settled, he met with her to find out how he could support her and her team. During the meeting, she said to him, "I'm so glad you are here to help us, I am eager to see what strategy you have for us to move forward on these goals." He replied, "Oh, my role isn't to design a strategy for you, it is to help you to design your own strategy and where appropriate, to help you execute on it. I can also provide you with guidance on approaches to help you be successful along the way." She paused. After a long moment she said, "Well, I'm not sure where we are supposed to get the strategy, if you don't design it. We don't have expertise on inclusion here." My client worked to help clarify his role as supporther and the new leader continued to suggest that she couldn't create a strategy, and he should probably do it for her team. Feeling the pressure from the discussion, he ended the meeting by saying, "I'm going to come back to you with a strategic plan for you to consider."

To be clear, his job isn't to build strategy for the team he's supporting. His role is to help give guidance as they design their own strategy that works with the kind of work they do, and to provide support and accountability on delivering their strategy. Yet there he was in their conversation, passively agreeing to do work he technically doesn't have the ability or responsibility to do. When I asked him why he agreed to take on creating the strategy, he said, "I am responsible for holding her accountable for her strategy and I don't want to be in trouble when I have nothing because she didn't give me anything. Also, she is new, but she is well liked, so I was afraid to challenge her."

Yikes.

People-pleasing will have you picking up balls someone else dropped that do not belong to you. Don't do it.

What follows are some techniques for how to speak up for yourself, stay out of people-pleasing, and not pick up balls that do not belong to you, all without destroying your reputation.

OPTION I

"It seems like there's some confusion with how we partner; can you help me understand where I can better clarify?"

Why this works:

This line of questioning takes the pressure off of you to explain and instead places the pressure on the person who is attempting to take advantage of you to be more explicit about their objectives. Rarely will a person taking advantage of someone else actually clarify their objectives. The person will likely say something like "I'm not confused" and you can respond with, "Oh, great – so we are on the same page that your role is _____ and mine is _____. I was concerned you were asking me to take on something that rests with your team." And just like that, the roles are clear.

OPTION II

"I think you are asking for me to do _____. That's technically outside of my scope of work/availability, but if you need assistance with how to _____, I am sure together we can find someone who can help."

Why this works:

This approach allows you to clearly share your boundaries, but still offer support to get whatever needs to be done, executed.

OPTION III

"Unfortunately, I won't be able to take that on/support in that way. I cannot do that because [explain why you cannot do what is being asked].

Why this works:

This approach defines your boundaries and explains the limits you are working within. If this is a work scenario like the one shared earlier in this section, it can give you an opportunity to highlight the long-term impacts of the other person's not delivering. So that might sound like "I cannot do that because I don't know enough about your business area to write a strategy for you independently. I can let my leadership know that you don't think you can hit the goals and see if they have any recommendations."

People-pleasing will keep you bound to your current position and role as well as create opportunities for resentment because it prolongs the issue at hand. In fact, with the client I was coaching, his agreement to "come back with something" set him up to have to set boundaries and define role clarity after he'd already violated them by taking on the task, that is, picking up the ball when it wasn't his to pick up. That means that in addition to the issue of role clarity still being an outstanding matter, there was now also a potential for the leader to feel misled and attempt to hold my client accountable for failing to deliver. Should my client decide to actually attempt to design the strategy, he is setting himself up to have a grudge against the leader for not delivering her work as well as him potentially having to take feedback from her on work he wasn't supposed to be doing.

If the ball isn't yours, don't touch it. Let it drop if you must. Instead, role-model what it looks like to advocate for yourself, your time, and your reputation.

15 Dealing with Professional Gaslighting

There have been times that I asked some powerful questions and rather than answer me, the person would gaslight me or attempt to sow seeds of doubt. Gaslighting is when someone makes you question reality and doubt your own memory or perceptions. It is abusive and if you are dealing with someone who gaslights you professionally, my biggest recommendation is to find a healthier work situation. Easier said than done, so I will cover a few ways to navigate when someone gaslights you professionally until you determine you can move on.

When dealing with a gaslighter, make sure the focal point is clear. Gaslighters will often try to redirect you away from the topic at hand, often to something that will upset you to take the attention off themselves. Don't allow it. When the gaslighter tries to redirect the conversation, say, "I appreciate that you want to discuss other topics, but at this time, I want to focus on this." Let them have a fit, try to derail, and feign being emotional if they must. You maintain your cool, and keep the topic at hand in focus; otherwise, you are wasting time.

Avoid interacting with the gaslighter one-on-one. Often gaslighters fly under the radar because they deny behaviors and it can put you in the situation of it being your word against theirs. Try to always have someone present when you have to interact with the gaslighter so there is another person who was a witness to the conversation. If you cannot avoid one-on-one contact, then make sure after each meeting to email them a recap of what was said – copy a colleague if it makes sense. This technique keeps a paper trail should you need to reference it and the emails will align with the dates of the interactions.

Gaslighters sometimes will throw in enough positive reinforcement to make you feel like they are improving their behavior or maybe lead you to believe that their bad behavior was just them having a bad day.

Be prepared for a rush of kindness after a gaslighter has acted out and prepare yourself for them to take all that positivity away and lash out at you at their convenience again later. The unfortunate thing about a gaslighter is that they tend to operate on a cycle of being amazing and then abusive. There is no stopping them. You can ask all the powerful questions and try to negotiate, but they will continue. If you want gaslighting to stop, you have to be willing to leave them or the collaborative situation altogether. In the meantime, try not to take anything personally.

There was a person in my life who was a gaslighter, and I am embarrassed to say the lengths I went to in an effort to try to keep things level in our friendship. He is incredibly smart and runs a couple of pretty well-known multimillion-dollar companies. He has at times been a great mentor and given me amazing advice over the 20 years I have known him. None of his advice was worth the gaslighting. He'd go into fits about how terribly I was running my company or how poorly I was communicating. At one point he ghosted me for a year because I didn't understand an agreement he wanted to sign with me where he would own part of my business. He would gaslight me over meetings he blew off or commitments he made: "Did we have a meeting or are you making that up?" There were several times we would not be on speaking terms and he would find a way to get us back to speaking – I mean everything from sending me flowers to sending me business. While I was writing this book he randomly blew off a dinner meeting we had, and I'd had enough. I blocked him on the spot. I have known that man 20-plus years. I know I will see him heading up some company, or he will be running for mayor one day in our hometown, and I will hear all about it. Based on his past patterns, he will likely try to make his way back into my life again, but I will never, ever speak to him again. I do miss the good times, his help and guidance, but the gaslighting was never worth it. I'd rather have my peace instead.

16 Saying No While Still Protecting Your Reputation

We have all heard it before: "No" is a complete sentence. That sentiment doesn't seem as useful when we are wanting to use our "no" in an environment where how people receive us has a big impact on our lives. Your reputation is incredibly important to how you experience your whole life. Folks receive (or don't receive) opportunities based on their reputation alone, so our instinct to want to protect our reputation is warranted. Agreeing to do something you don't want to, are not able to take on without undue burden, or just don't have the skillset to lead is not a good way to secure our reputations, either, but in the moment, a yes can feel like the best response when the ask is coming from a leader or an authority figure who can have some degree of influence over our experience.

In Chapter 11, Performative Allyship and Advocacy, I talked about how some organizations have been asking passionate but underrepresented leaders to take on the company's diversity, equity, and inclusion initiatives – often without any additional budget or human capital to assist with the work. I have so many folks, almost all of them Black women, who have reached out to me with an ask that sounds like this:

> I am the only Black woman on my senior leadership team –
> in fact, I am one of very few senior Black women leaders
> in the company. Because I recognize I have a different per-
> spective than many of my peers, I do make a pointed effort
> to highlight to my team opportunities when we can be more
> inclusive. Recently, I was asked to take on diversity and
> inclusion as a function. I am already full with my current
> workload and diversity and inclusion is not my area of exper-
> tise. How do I say no without it damaging my reputation,
> especially since I am the only Black woman on the team?

Here are a couple of options for how you can say no to asks for you to take on work that doesn't align with your skillset or bandwidth:

OPTION I

"I appreciate you considering me for this and I care just as much as you do about our succeeding in the work of inclusion. However, diversity and inclusion work is not my functional area of expertise and with my current workload, I don't think I have the capacity to get skilled up in a way that would be most impactful for the company's goals. My recommendation would be to hire someone with the skillset we need to take this on and really win at it. What are your thoughts?"

Why this works:

This response pulls in the asker as a partner instead of just a colleague or possible superior. This approach also thanks the asker for considering you, which acknowledges that they gave the ask some thought (whether they did or not really doesn't matter). Prefacing your decline with these two sentiments helps the asker to hear your decline as thoughtful and intentional instead of resistant. Adding in your recommendation at the end also shows that you are invested in things going well even if you are not personally involved.

OPTION II

"Oh! I am surprised that you are asking me to take on diversity and inclusion work, given it is not my area of expertise. Can you share why you think I am an ideal fit for this work?" When they offer an answer (which will likely be about you demonstrating care and passion for the work), you can reply with, "Thank you so much for considering me, but I think you and I both equally share a passion for this work! As we have both witnessed, for inclusion and equity work to be successful, it requires so much more than passion; it needs time and expertise. I am happy to make some recommendations of some folks who might be a good fit to help us. Have you considered this as a full-time position or an opportunity to bring in a consultant?"

Why this works:

This approach invites the asker to consider why they asked you and to share the reason with you. Hearing someone's reason for asking provides an opportunity for you to connect with them on a personal level, which can soften the no. Asking why someone considered you is a good way to hold the asker accountable to be thoughtful about why they are taking the actions they are instead of just operating without consideration.

While your instincts may cause your tone to come across as being a bit put off at someone asking you to do a job that isn't in alignment with your skillset, especially if you think it could be tied to how you identify in some way, push that instinct aside. It's likely all speculation and difficult to validate. Instead, be purposeful and message your decline in a tone that says what your language says: you are happy to be considered and although you aren't the right person, you still want the outcome to be favorable.

Sometimes we just need to know how to say no in general. I have found that people are particularly triggered by the word no, so I rarely use it, and when I do, I frame it strategically. I am not passive aggressive; I will clearly decline, I just use words that are less likely to trigger someone, since there are so many ways to say no without using the actual word.

Here is a formula I often will use to help me say no without being offensive:

1. React positively and appreciately that you were invited or considered. The first reaction sets the tone for the rest of the conversation. This might sound like:
   - Oh, wow, thanks for thinking of me!
   - I appreciate that you have noticed my passion for _____.
   - Thank you for considering me for such an important/exciting opportunity/event.
   - I appreciate you asking!
2. Weave in a point of shared connection or interest. This might sound like:
   - I think we both know how important _____ is.

- I know we both understand how challenging/exciting/etc. _____ can be.
- I think we both have observed that _____ can require concerted time and attention to be successful.

3. Decline the ask. This is where the "no" happens and it can sound like:
    - Unfortunately, I'm not able to take that on at this time.
    - I'm not sure I am a good fit for this opportunity with my current workload/skillset.
    - I won't be able to accommodate that in my schedule.
    - I am not going to be able to attend.
4. Close with a question or, if you are so inclined, an offer to assist. This might sound like:
    - Would you like some recommendations for _____?
    - What's your perspective on _____ as an alternative?
    - Have you considered _____?

You can use this formula to say no to friends, colleagues, family, or pretty much anyone. Let go of the idea that saying no has to be aggressive or angry. Instead, view saying no as opening up space for opportunities that are a better fit for you and for the person who is asking. Of course, there are going to be times that someone is going to challenge your no. Don't let guilt be the reason you say yes. In fact, sometimes I will playfully ask, "Are you trying to make me feel bad because I am saying no?" and most folks will back off after that. No one wants to be called out for being pushy or peer pressuring someone to do something they can't or don't want to do.

Sometimes you will be the recipient of a no, and fear of a no can often keep people from asking for things. Those who do not ask often go without. Just think about how often you have done something just because someone asked you. There is no harm in asking for what you want, whether that is days off, a career opportunity, a network connection, or a raise. There is no harm in a respectful ask. In fact, you may find that someone has something else to offer that might be just as good or greater than what you asked for. Speaking up also applies to asking for what you want in your career.

Speaking Up: At Home, at Work, in the World, with Friends, and to Experts

The next several chapters are dedicated entirely to giving you actual scripts and language you can use when you want to speak up. They are broken down into a few specific kinds of experiences; specifically, I cover intimidation, navigating a power imbalance, feeling disrespected, being isolated, being blamed, being dismissed, medical advocacy, and being interrupted. I offer what a person can say speaking up for themselves as well as some options for speaking up as an ally for each experience. Some of the experiences touch on a few different issues all in one conversation, and you may find there is symmetry in the language. The goal here isn't to overwhelm you with sentences to use, but to give you some good frameworks for the language of speaking up at home, at work, in the world, with friends, and to experts. Everything you have read up to this point in this book was intended to help you to have all the tools you need to be able to do what this part of the book asks you to do: effectively speak up for yourself and others.

Let's lean into some experiences that often call for us to push back and speak up for ourselves and others.

17

Intimidation: But What If They Know More Than I Do?

An obstacle to some folks' speaking up is their personal perception that the speaker is either smarter than them or is speaking (intentionally or unintentionally) above their level of understanding. This can happen with medical professionals or other experts we encounter. Here's the thing – it might be uncomfortable, but if you notice something a professional or an expert misses, or you are not following along with the information being shared, or even if you just know that something is going unaddressed, it is imperative for you to speak up. Remember, being inclusive means we have to bring everyone along – you can't follow along and get what you need out of the situation if the message is being lost. If you have this challenge, I encourage you to push past the emotions you may have around seeming uninformed or unable to keep up and to instead say something! I know, you may be a bit nervy about potentially putting yourself in a position of looking silly or being made an example of, or sounding uninformed. With the right phrasing, all of those experiences are avoidable. Following are a few scripts you can use to speak up in this kind of situation. Remember, you can always tailor a script to work best for you.

OPTION I

"My apologies for interrupting, I'm concerned I am not following along. Can you clarify what you mean when you said [insert idea here]?"

Why this works:

This approach allows you to ask the speaker a question that invites them to show more of their knowledge. For a person eager to show off (as many folks who talk above our heads are eager to do), it invites them to do more of that and also helps you get an answer to your questions.

OPTION II

"Thank you for taking your time and explaining this to me/us. I have a few thoughts. Do you mind taking a few minutes to answer some questions to make sure I am following along?"

Why this works:

This question shows appreciation to the speaker and creates an opportunity for you to ask any probing questions. It is framed in a way that would make it a challenge to say no to because it makes it clear they would knowingly be leaving you with a gap in your understanding if they decline to answer your questions.

OPTION III

"I think I understand. Do you mind if I repeat back to you what I heard so you can let me know if we are on the same page?"

Why this works:

This question invites the speaker to join you at your level of understanding. By you asking to repeat what the speaker said, you are inviting the speaker to become the listener and to let them hear what you understood in your language. Most folks will adapt to communicating in a way that you will better understand.

Make sure you turn your curiosity on with these questions, as we discussed in Part II of this book. People should be able to palpably perceive curiosity in your tone of voice and your body language.

Sometimes we witness intimidation as an ally, and speaking up is important in these circumstances as well. I can remember many years ago I was in a car repair place with an older vehicle and the repair people called me to take a look at my car. They proceeded to explain to me what was happening to my car while arbitrarily pointing at various points of the underside of the vehicle. I can't even recall what was wrong, but I was led to believe that I had to make a call on the car pretty immediately because I might not even make it home. I went back into the waiting area and called my best guy friend at the time to share with him what was going on and get his take on the situation. A older Black man sitting not far from me could hear my conversation and when I hung up the call he said, "Excuse me, young lady, would you mind telling me what they told you was wrong with your car?" I explained to him what I was told and he asked me what kind of car I had. I told him and he said, "I am not sure that's what your car needs, but I know cars pretty well. When they come back out here, are you okay with letting me do the talking?" I nodded. A few minutes later the repairperson came to ask me how I wanted to proceed and the stranger who offered to help piped up. He began asking questions and I could see that the repairperson was confused by what had happened. By the end of the exchange, I was able to get a pretty minor repair done and was well on my way.

I was intimidated by the knowledge the repairperson had and the man in the waiting room, clearly having a better working knowledge of cars, was able to step in and keep me from having to pay for things I did not need. When we are in a position where we can see someone is intimidated and we understand what is happening, we can lean in as an ally to support them. What follows are a few techniques you can use to interrupt intimidation.

OPTION I

"Can you help me understand why you are taking that approach to address this concern? I think I have a good recommendation, but I want to make sure I understand completely."

Why this works:

This framing puts the intimidator on the hook to be accountable for their actions and levels the playing field, because suddenly the intimidator is communicating with someone who understands what is going on instead of someone who is feeling uncertain about their level of understanding.

OPTION II

"I'm not sure that's the best approach, have you considered [insert alternate approach here]?"

Why this works:

Similar to the first approach, this framing lets the intimidator know that someone else understands the subject matter. It also makes a recommendation for the intimidator to react to.

When you are serving as an ally, you do not want to just jump into folks' personal business unless someone is in physical danger. Did you notice how the man in the car repair place who offered to help me asked me first? He led with "Excuse me, young lady, would you mind telling me what they told you was wrong with your car?" so I could invite him in. Allies can make the mistake of jumping into things that folks are not looking for help with and they don't have the full context. Make sure to ask if you can help and wait to be invited. Asking helps keep you informed and protects you from offending someone or coming across as trying to be a savior.

18 Power Imbalance: What If I Am Not the One with the Power?

We discussed the role power can play in our speaking up in Chapter 9, Why Is Pushing Back So Hard? Perceiving that someone has some power over us can make us silent because we don't want to deal with any adverse impact from speaking up. Just because someone has the power doesn't mean that they are someone we cannot speak up with. We covered how to speak up with your leader in Chapter 10, Critical Communication Tools. Let's explore a couple of scenarios here to help you speak up to be treated equitably when there is a power imbalance.

Scenario I: Store Associate/Child

After a great week at school, Carrie promises her children ice cream. She pulls up to the local parlor and sends her two sons, 10 and 12, into the ice cream shop. She tells them to get what they want and to grab her a small vanilla milkshake. When they come back, Carrie notices that the milkshake is not full and the boys' ice cream scoops are light. She asks the boys if they said anything, and they both say no, but they acknowledge that they did notice that the portions didn't seem right. What could Carrie or her sons say to speak up? Yes, even the children could have spoken up.

OPTION I

"I notice that this scoop is smaller than the last time I was here/my mom brought us here for ice cream. Would you mind checking and adding add a bit more to my serving, please?"

OPTION II

"I/My mom really love(s) the milkshakes here. This one seems half full. Can you check it for me before I take it?"

Why these work:

This approach lets the employee of the shop know that you have an expectation because of past experience and asks them to fix it to align with your previous standard. If the children say it, these approaches also let the shopkeeper know another authority figure is involved by mentioning that Mom is nearby. Kids have a natural sort of innocence and curiosity that can make it easier for people not to be offended as long as the kids are not rude.

Scenario II: Favored Associate/Less Known Associate

Corey has been working at Amazing Home Repair store almost since the store opened; in fact, he was employee number three. Everyone knows and enjoys him, and he is friendly with everyone. Corey consistently mispronounces TaKiyah's name. She smiles and corrects him quietly, but he never gets it right. You aren't sure he is trying. One day as she is leaving, he waves, and then looks over at you and says, "I don't know why they would name someone like that, it is so hard. Why can't folks just give their kids simple names?" How can you speak up as an ally for TaKiyah?

OPTION I

"Let's consider for a moment that perhaps TaKiyah's name is not hard, but instead that you are uniquely challenged by it. You seem to get along with her, and someone's name is really important to their identity. Are you willing to practice saying TaKiyah's name correctly?"

OPTION II

"Yikes. How would you feel if someone told you that your name was hard? I think you can get TaKiyah's name right if you try. Are you willing to practice saying it correctly?"

Why these work:

Both approaches help highlight that names are an important part of identity, which most folks will agree with. People want to be called by their names and will usually agree that they should call someone else by their correct name and be willing to work on it.

If instead of being an ally, you are the person whose name is being mispronounced, there are a couple ways you could speak up.

OPTION I

"I notice that you pronounce my name incorrectly. Can I teach you how to properly pronounce it?"

OPTION II

"My name means a lot to me and I try to take care to pronounce it so people can hear how to say it clearly. Would you like for me to pronounce it more slowly for you so you can practice saying it correctly?"

Why these work:

Both approaches enroll the person who is saying the name incorrectly into practicing saying it properly. This approach also makes it easier for someone to correct the other person in the moment because you've had the shared experience of saying the name correctly, together. Accountability for proper pronunciation would naturally follow.

Though the circumstance might be frustrating, try to ask these questions with an inviting tone, as if you are asking a friend to join you for a cup of coffee. There is absolutely a place for frustration when someone continues to mispronounce your name, but it should surface only after there has been some deliberate correction such as the options presented here.

19 Microaggressions: What If I Am Encountering a Microaggression?

Microaggressions is a term that falls under a broader category of behavior called micromessaging. Micromessaging includes several other terms like microinequities, microinsults, microaffirmations, and microinvalidations. What all these terms have in common is that they are indicated by small behaviors, which is what the prefix *micro-* suggests. While I am sharing a few of the terms that fall under micromessaging, keep in mind that many times any micromessage will be referred to as a microaggression by most people, and the specificity of the term isn't as important as understanding how micromessages present in our encounters with others and what the behaviors associated with them suggest.

Microaggressions are small or subtle behaviors that occur in casual encounters that judge, accuse, demean, marginalize, or show prejudice toward someone. They are experienced as minor verbal or nonverbal actions that can discount a person, single someone out, or belittle someone based on a part of their identity such as age, race, or gender. Microaggressions can be deliberate or unintentional.

Microaggressions are small behaviors, but they are considered aggressive because of the frequency that the recipient of the microaggression experiences them. The impact of microaggressions is cumulative. When someone encounters the same small slight over and over, it feels more impactful each time it happens. The microaggression could be something as simple as people routinely mispronouncing your name. After a while it might feel frustrating. People might even minimize your pushing back by saying something like, "Your name is so hard to pronounce," and then continuing to call you by the wrong name. The act itself is small, but the frequency of the experience makes it feel aggressive to the receiver. Another issue with microaggressions is that the receiver of the same microaggression over and over can get so fed up over time that they could ultimately take their frustration out on someone who innocently commits the microaggression who has no context or awareness of the history behind the "micro" behavior.

Likely you have heard of microaggressions and may even be familiar with a couple of common ones, like suggesting that someone Asian is "good at math," which reinforces a stereotype that all Asian people are good at math. Another common one is asking a tall person, especially a Black man, if they play basketball, which reinforces the stereotype that any tall Black men must be good at sports. It is also possible that you have tried to learn about microaggressions by memorizing what you learn to be offensive, or by avoiding engaging with a diverse group of folks in general. Memorizing microaggressions isn't the best approach. Certainly, you should keep in mind common remarks that can be offensive, but because micromessages are cultural and subjective, and there will be different ones in different parts of the world, the best approach is to be open to correction when you offend, and ready to apologize for the offense. "I apologize for assuming you are good at math. Moving forward I will not rely on stereotypes when interacting with people."

If you experience a microaggression, you should speak up. Folks don't always know they are being offensive, and can only learn if they are told. Additionally, often folks' comments are framed from their perspective and they are not considerate of the impact of their words. Avoiding speaking up about microaggressions allows the culprit to continue to behave in ways that can be offensive and it encourages us to suppress our feelings about poor behavior. Let's explore a couple of examples that include microaggressions.

An article by Edith Cooper was published in the opinion section of the *New York Times* entitled, "I Was Told I Have Career Advantages 'as a Black Woman.' Here's How I Replied."[1] In the article, a Black woman describes being told by a White male colleague that he had no chance of being able to join a corporate board because boards are looking for Black

---

[1] Edith Cooper, "I Was Told I Have Career Advantages 'as a Black Woman.' Here's How I Replied." *New York Times*, November 2, 2021, https://www.nytimes.com/2021/11/02/opinion/culture/board-diversity-black-women.html.

women. The author writes that her colleague said, "Edith, you must be in great demand – as a Black woman." This microaggressive statement suggests that regardless of how qualified and competent Edith is, she will get board opportunities because she is a Black woman. The author offers one approach in the article (I encourage you to take a moment to read the article because it is focused on more than just the microaggression), but let's explore some potential simple responses to this kind of microaggression.

OPTION I

Press for more information about the part that was microaggressive: "Can you share more about what you mean by 'as a Black woman'?"

OPTION II

Highlight your desire for more clarity: "I am not sure I follow what you are suggesting, and I don't want to assume. Can you elaborate?"

OPTION III

Repeat what you heard back to them as a question so they can hear how it sounds: "It sounds like you think I am getting an opportunity that you will not simply because I am a Black woman. Am I understanding that correctly?"

Why these work:

Asking a question about what you just heard puts the responsibility back on the person who made the microaggressive statement to clarify it. Most folks will hear the offense in their statements when you query them and will correct themselves.

Of course, there is a possibility the person you are speaking with will double down on their perspective or they might make a statement like

"I didn't mean to offend you." In such cases, you can take a couple of additional steps:

- If the relationship is valuable to you, open with, "Thanks for sharing your perspective with me so I understand" or a sentiment that recognizes the person's willingness to be candid. You may not like or appreciate their perspective, but they also could have declined to share it with you. If you aren't concerned about the relationship, this is less important.
- Say, "I'm not sure you understand how offensive your statement comes across. Are you open to hearing my perspective?" Most folks will say yes. If they say no, discontinue the discussion altogether with a statement like, "I understand. Well, it's probably best we change the subject." If someone indicates an unwillingness to listen, you are under no obligation to force them, and they likely will not hear you, anyway.
- If the person has said something along the lines of "No offense," then you can say, "I didn't say you offended me. I would like an answer to my question, though. I think there is an opportunity for us to have an important discussion here if you are willing to continue to respectfully engage." Most folks will appreciate your interest and will lean into the discussion.

Addressing microaggressions as an ally is a bit more delicate. Usually, I recommend that an ally only chime in if the microaggression is either very blatant or offensive; if it is in an environment you are familiar with the nuances of; or you have had an opportunity to check in with the person experiencing the microaggression (either before or after it has happened) to know where they stand on it. Otherwise you could be chiming in on a personal matter that is not really an allyship opportunity at all. Let's explore an example of how an ally might address a microaggression.

My mentee's former job was at an predominantly White college and most of her colleagues were White. Like many colleges, when the pandemic hit, her department went virtual for work. The college also decided in the summer of 2020 that they should have some diversity training in light of the racial reckoning happening across the company. During a meeting, my mentee, who is a Black woman, logged in like usual to join what was the third session in a series of diversity trainings. Over the weekend, my mentee had changed her hair and was wearing it in a short style highlighting her natural hair texture. A White female colleague who had never spoken to her before piped up shortly after logging in and said, "Oh, Kennedy! I see you changed your hair! Do you like it?" Kennedy paused a moment, feeling deeply offended at "Do you like it?" and simply said yes, then turned her camera off and started to cry.

Noticing the exchange, and realizing it was in the middle of a diversity and inclusion training, Kennedy's leader, who has a good relationship with Kennedy, spoke up as an ally. "Ellen, 'Do you like it?' is an interesting reaction to someone changing their hair. I don't think you know Kennedy. Can you share why 'Do you like it?' felt like the right approach?"

Ellen was immediately embarrassed and said simply, "My apologies, I didn't mean anything by it, I just noticed that her hair was different."

Kennedy's leader spoke again. "I think you can probably appreciate that when you make a change to your appearance, the last reaction you are looking for from a complete stranger is 'Do you like it?' Perhaps in the future, you will consider the appropriateness of your personal remarks on someone's appearance."

Notice how Kennedy's leader simply asked a question to hold Ellen accountable for her words: "Can you share why 'Do you like it?' felt like the right approach?" Ellen immediately shifted her approach, realizing that "Do you like it?" was as inappropriate as saying, "I don't like your hair." As the leader, Kennedy's superior had the credibility to speak up and garner the respect of the others in the room. Remember, allyship often requires us to take a moment and recognize where we have influence that others in the room may not. Ellen and many others may not know that Black women's hairstyles are an aspect of identity that is often met with microaggressions. In fact, at the time of this writing, 12 states have passed what's known as the CROWN Act, legislation designed to ban race-based hair discrimination. That's the thing about microaggressions—often folks don't know they're perpetrating them, but just like when we spot poor behaviors in children, correction can go a long way.

Following are a couple of other ways an ally could speak up about microaggressive behavior:

OPTION I

"We are focused on creating an inclusive experience and your remark could be perceived as offensive. Can we commit to being more thoughtful and responsible about how we communicate with those on our team?"

Why this works:

This highlights that the behavior is not appropriate for an inclusive environment and that an inclusive experience is of value for the team or workplace.

OPTION II

"I'm sure you have the best intentions, but I don't think your approach/question is respectful. We can discuss offline a bit later, but perhaps we should turn our attention to our agenda."

Why this works:

You quickly address the behavior, setting the expectation for anyone else around that it is unacceptable and also message that there will be some followup. Most folks want to know that someone who has been microaggressive will learn why what they said was offensive and, potentially, even apologize for it.

While both of the examples presented in this section involve Black women, please note that microaggressions can be committed to any identity. One behavior that people do not always recognize as microaggressive is misgendering people. Folks who use nonbinary pronouns like they, hir, xe, or others are perpetually misgendered, so the experience piles on and can create frustration. If you use pronouns other than he or she, I know it is frustrating, but I implore you to speak up when you have the bandwidth to do so. As the world is experiencing a mindset shift to make the space for your identity in the world that you have always deserved, you are shouldering the bruises of global growth. Here are a few ways I recommend you push back or speak up when you are called by the wrong pronoun aside from the typical light correction you've commonly seen.

OPTION I

Turn on your curiosity and sincerely ask, "Who were you referring to when you said, 'she'?"

Why this works:

It puts the burden and discomfort on the person who misgendered you and likely will encourage them to be more mindful of their language in the future. The key here is to be genuinely confused rather than offended. Offense puts people on the defense; confusion holds people accountable to find a solve.

OPTION II

"I notice you keep misgendering me and I imagine it would make you uncomfortable if I were to continue calling you by someone else's name. Are you open to me making a few recommendations on how you can practice using appropriate pronouns?" If their answer is yes, I encourage you to share any resources you feel comfortable sharing. I often tell people who want to reprogram the mental muscle around pronouns to commit to using nonbinary pronouns for everyone for one week a month. It builds the practice of awareness into how people communicate.

Why this works:

It calls out the behavior and offers a solution for the person to change their behavior. This approach does require some degree of intimate labor, so you may want to reserve this approach for someone you have a vested interest in a long-term relationship with.

OPTION III

"I'm curious; when you misgender me, how do you recommend I address it?"

Why this works:

Very simply, this approach takes the labor off of you by making the person who is misgendering you do the labor of figuring out how to address the issue. Should the person say they don't have a recommendation, you can ask if you can offer one. If someone simply says it is too hard, ask them, "How would you feel if I told you pronouncing your name is too hard?" Most folks can then see how their approach needs to shift.

Microaggressions happen very often, and they are not the same across communities or across the world. They are largely subjective and circumstantial, as is most of life. The nuances matter when it comes to interpreting an experience. Remember to be open to correction at all times, because we do not always have the full context or understand the cultural nuances of the environment we are engaging in.

20 Disrespected: What If Someone Is Blatantly Mistreating Me or Crossing a Line?

Blatant and intentional disrespectful behaviors are sometimes the hardest to speak up against because they can catch us off guard. We generally expect that people will not be deliberately rude or inappropriate with us, so when it happens we may find ourselves at a loss for words. Most of us know blatant disrespect when it happens; we feel it in our bodies – a racing heart, anger, sweaty palms, or whatever your body does to let you know someone has crossed a line. A lot of us shrink. We stuff it down, we boil under our skin, and we rant about it to our friends, sometimes spouting off what we wish we had said. Let's explore a couple of blatantly disrespectful encounters and some techniques to address them.

My friend Lauren was walking to her car from the mall one afternoon. As she passed a group of men, one of them started catcalling her. "Aye, shorty. You fine as hell. Why don't you come bring that body over here?" She looked at him directly and said, "Really? Is that what we are doing today? Harassing women on the way to their cars? Do you talk to the women you care about like that?" The man stopped cold, lowered his voice and immediately apologized, "I'm sorry. You're right. My bad, no disrespect." Lauren continued on to her car.

Confidently addressing inappropriate behavior usually works. In this scenario, Lauren didn't miss a beat. She was in her own neighborhood and felt confident speaking up in a way that let the man speaking to her know she wasn't interested and that his approach was inappropriate. The fact is that most people do not expect others to project confidence or to speak up for themselves. Most people would have averted their eyes and ignored the man catcalling, and likely, feeling that he had the upper hand, he would have continued as long as she was in earshot. By confidently addressing the man, she robbed him of the power he felt catcalling her. She also was in her own neighborhood, so she spoke to him in a casual tone of voice and using language he culturally could understand. Our abilities to engage in our many diverse communities are not tools to cast aside. There are situations where they can give us confidence and the language we need to speak up.

Blatant disrespect happens in the office as well. Let's explore an example I raised in Chapter 9: Nicol is a Black woman managing a White woman named Sue in an office environment. Though Nicol is more senior, Sue has been at the company for 15 years compared to Nicol's 2 years, so she knows everyone there. Sue is routinely disrespectful to Nicol. One morning she stormed into Nicol's office and yelled at her, "Stop sending me emails first thing in the morning! I am just getting my day started!" and stormed off, slamming the door behind her. Another time Sue snapped at Nicol in the middle of Nicol giving her some directions. "I guess you just won't help me with anything!" Nicol has been silently tolerating Sue's outbursts because she feels like she is one of the few Black people there and doesn't want to be seen as an "angry Black woman." Nicol also thinks Sue believes she is older than Nicol even though they are the same age. How can Nicol address Sue's blatant disrespect and not damage her own reputation?

OPTION I

The next time Sue has a disrespectful outburst, Nicol should walk away and make a note of it. At their next encounter, Nicol should calmly say, "During our last conversation, you had an inappropriate outburst. That style of communication is not an effective way to engage with me. Are you willing to engage responsibly in this conversation?" Sue will likely be caught off guard. She could apologize or she could have another outburst. If the latter happens, Nicol should go with her documentation to Human Resources.

Why this works:

This approach lets Sue know that her behavior is inappropriate and sets the expectation for how she should behave going forward by inviting her to engage differently. It also creates a documentation trail for Nicol's records if necessary.

OPTION II

Nicol can calmly say to Sue, "My expectation as a leader in this organization and on this team is that we will work to be respectful in our communication with one another to uphold the company values. I'd like to discuss some concerns I have with how you engage with me and the rest of the team." Again, Sue might be caught off guard. She could get defensive, or she might be willing to have the discussion. In either case, Nicol should document the discussion for her records.

Why this works:

This approach establishes the roles that Nicol and Sue should play in the organization and the expectations of each person in their roles. Leaders should always find a way to tie expectations back to the values of the company. This way, Nicol can easily help Sue to see why her behavior does not align with the organization, and she can document the behavior change (or lack thereof) that she notices in Sue.

Everyone needs allies to step in when someone is being mistreated or blatantly disrespected. If you notice someone is being mistreated or disrespected, at the very least you can chime in and simply ask, "Why are you treating them that way?" This applies to when you see someone being treated differently than you in a department store, in a work meeting, or in a grocery store parking lot. This simple question lets folks know that their behavior is out of line and that someone is willing to push back against it. Remember, many people of varying identities take disrespect because they believe that they have to and they don't want to deal with the consequences of speaking up, which can include putting their job at risk, ruining their reputation, getting arrested, or being further attacked. Often, allies don't run the same risk. If you find yourself in the position to be an ally because the risk you face for speaking up is less than that of the person facing the mistreatment, use your privilege by being willing to speak up.

The key with addressing blatant disrespect is not to shrink as if you are deserving of the disrespectful behavior. Some folks have been bullying people their whole lives and they continue because it is rare for anyone to directly address their behavior. Always remember that you deserve to be respected; it is not optional. Your approach should always be calm and confident when addressing disrespect, and if the other person's behavior does not allow space for that kind of approach, you should remove yourself until it does. The bigger and angrier you behave, the more you are feeding the disrespectful person energy to act out – do them no such favor. Only be willing to engage when they are behaving appropriately.

21 Underrepresented: What If I Am the Only One?

Lots of times we are the only one – the only woman, the only Asian person, even if you are the only White person – in a space and we feel really uncomfortable speaking up. Being the only in a situation can make us question whether we should assert ourselves or stay silent to blend in and be seen as a "team player." Being underrepresented in a room can make us quiet, but remember, some folks are underrepresented in everyday life. That can mean that, for these folks, the shrinking and not speaking up can become a part of how they survive and not call too much attention to themselves. This feeling can be exacerbated when some aspect of their identity is subject to stereotypes. It is going to feel hard, but when you are the only one, in some ways it is even more important that you speak up. You might have a unique perspective that might otherwise go unnoticed if you do not, or you might be subjecting yourself to unfair treatment that can wear you out from holding in it over time.

In Chapter 8, Overcoming the Most Common Obstacles, I told you about Brandon and me at a Starbucks in a mall one day where the barista messed up his drink order. Although the order was not right, he was not going to say anything because he is a "six-foot-four, 240-pound Black man" and he always reminds me that many of the baristas are "usually women who are often much smaller than I am and often White," to use his words. "I just don't want to be the big Black guy in the room complaining about my drink and it all goes wrong and I end up in handcuffs." Some of you may be reading this and think it sounds extreme, but he has been living in his body a long time and pays attention to how Black men seemingly minding their own business can end up in life-threatening or dangerous situations.

That day, I ended up speaking to the barista to get Brandon's drink corrected. After we got our coffees, I told him that even when you are the only one or are concerned about the way someone might perceive you, it is incredibly important that you speak up. I asked him if he was open to some recommendations from me on approach. When he agreed, here is what I offered.

OPTION I

At a break in customers, approach the barista warmly and with grace. Make sure to use open body language and speak in an inviting tone (sort of how one might speak to an older woman you were holding the door for). Say to the barista, loud enough only for her to hear, but not quite a whisper, "My apologies for interrupting your process, but I think my drink is incorrect, can you help me?"

Why this works:

Warm and inviting is disarming, even when it comes from someone who might be what many see as a stereotype. Opening with the acknowledgment that you are interrupting what they are working on comes across as self-aware and considerate and will tend to make someone more inclined to be positively responsive. Ending the sentiment with a question puts the barista on the hook to respond – most will say yes or will find someone else who can assist.

It is important for me to share that I don't think it is fair or right that anyone should have to navigate how they come across out of concern for their identity. I do think knowing how to navigate the situation by making adjustments at least gives you an option, instead of feeling like silence is the only option.

Weeks later, Brandon had another encounter where he tried the approach I suggested, and it worked! It was a bit of a different circumstance, but the environment was the same – he was the only and was concerned that expressing a concern would create a big problem. He pushed that aside and did as I suggested and ended up having stellar service as a result.

Here is another example. José was in line to take a Covid test. He had attended an event and been notified that several folks at that event were positive, so he needed to get tested to return to work. While in line, he was six feet from the person he was in line behind, but the woman behind him, who had a toddler with her, wasn't maintaining social distancing and was very close to him. José was uncomfortable with her being so close. He didn't want to speak up because not only was he the only man in line, he was the only one who appeared to be Latino. "I was concerned that if I asked the woman behind me to back up some, she would be offended or feel like I was being aggressive, so I just made sure I wore my mask the whole time." After hearing the story, I here is how I suggested José approach the situation.

OPTION I

Turn to the woman and say in a warm and inviting tone, "Excuse me, ma'am, I know a lot of folks are here to get tested just for work, but I am concerned I have been exposed and I do not want to expose you or your child. Can we create some space between us and socially distance?"

Why this works:

Similar to the example with Brandon in the Starbucks, warm and inviting is disarming, even when it comes from someone who might be what many see as a stereotype. Opening with the acknowledgment that you are not accusing the person of having Covid comes across as self-aware and considerate and will tend to make someone more inclined to oblige without protest. Ending the sentiment with a question puts the woman on the hook to respond – which would most likely result in the woman and her child backing up.

If your fear of speaking up as the only one of your identity in a room is connected to not being seen as a team player, one tactic that works is to open the dialogue with your concern about not being seen as a member of the team. So say something like, "I am really committed to this team's success, so I want to share this because I want to make sure it doesn't derail us moving forward." Another approach could be, "I realize it is possible I am the only one who has this concern, but I want to make sure we are putting our best foot forward as a team." Lastly, you could say something like, "I am a little nervous about sharing this because I don't want to be seen as not being a team player. Are you open to hearing my concern?" This approach invites the person to be curious and feel accountable not to belittle you or your concern's value to the team.

Serving as an ally for someone who is in the position of being the only in the room can be a little tricky unless you already have a relationship with the person who is having the "only one" experience. I know Brandon well, so I noticed his disappointment in his drink order and his apprehension about speaking up. It was easy for me to lean in and help get the drink corrected and have a follow-up conversation with recommendations for him in the future. If you do not have this kind of relationship with someone but sense that they may be feeling the pressure of being the only one in the room, your best step is to always invite them to engage and work to create spaces that feel safe for them to speak up and push back. As a reminder, we discussed ways to create safe spaces in Chapter 8, Overcoming the Most Common Obstacles.

22

Dismissed: What If I Am Not Feeling Heard?

Sometimes not feeling like someone is listening can cause folks to stop speaking up in the moment and, depending on the situation, altogether. We have all had that moment of feeling frustrated because we aren't being heard. For some of you, the discomfort of even playing back in your mind the last time you didn't feel heard causes you to have that nervy uncomfortable feeling that happens somewhere between your nose and your navel.

I have a dear friend who, shortly after giving birth, began to have some severe pain in one of her breasts. Feeling exhausted and overwhelmed with the first few months of being a mom to a newborn, she casually mentioned it to me in a call and I said she needed to call her doctor. After a day or so of convincing, she called the doctor, who didn't have any appointments open until about a week out. I convinced her to set up a telehealth visit with her doctor's office to speak with a lactation nurse in the meantime. During the call, my friend explained to the nurse what her symptoms were, and the nurse said, "Well, I'm not sure what it is, but you can come in." My friend was so frustrated, she just withdrew. The nurse made no attempts to remotely evaluate her by asking probing questions or anything. The nurse also just seemed generally uninterested and disengaged. Who wants to deal with that while also battling a health concern and taking care of a new baby?

Feeling dismissed, my friend resigned to deal with the pain and fever she was suffering until the doctor's appointment rolled around a week or so later. When I talked to her, she was very uncomfortable and running a fever, so I couldn't believe how the doctor's office was treating her – and she was just going to let it happen! Why? "I mean they are the doctors. I told them what is happening, and they didn't seem concerned or even ask any follow-up questions. If they aren't worried, then I guess I shouldn't be, either." She felt dismissed and therefore wasn't speaking up for herself.

Let's go through some ways to speak up when we are feeling dismissed.

OPTION I

"Thank you for that information. I have some additional perspective to share, are you able to listen to my concerns at this time?"

Why this works:

This question invites the person dismissing you to listen. It purposely does not say, "you are not listening," because that statement will cause someone to be defensive and ultimately listen less. Instead, it asks to be heard.

OPTION II

"I appreciate what you have shared so far. I'm not sure I heard the solution clearly, can you explain what the next steps are again so I know what to do to get this addressed?"

Why this works:

Even if the person hasn't given you any next steps, this puts them on the hook to either do so or admit they do not know what to do. Either way, you have some information to help you determine what your next step is instead of just being confused. To be fair, the person may be aware that you are guiding them to give you a response, but so long as you message with an inviting tone, they are likely to comply.

OPTION III

"It sounds like you are frustrated, and I can understand how that can happen in this situation. I still have some unanswered questions. Is there someone else I can speak to who might be better able to assist at this time?"

Why this works:

It makes it clear that you notice there is a disconnect and that you are being treated poorly. Usually, the recipient of this message will get a little defensive and may say something like, "I am not frustrated," and then offer some more meaningful steps to take. Don't personalize the frustration at all. If the person harps on your pointing out your observations about their demeanor, you can say, "I understand. Thank you for letting me know my observation was incorrect. I appreciate you helping me," if you are so inclined.

Remember to mind your tone here. When you are having the experience of being dismissed, it's easy to move into frustration yourself. Instead, lean into more of an upbeat, confused tone, as though you are generally having a fantastic day and you really don't understand why you are being dismissed – which honestly is probably true; we often have no idea why people are being dismissive, and we don't need to. What we need to do is execute toward our objective without being infected by someone else's mood.

For those of you who are wondering how my friend turned out, she actually had a pretty severe case of mastitis. I was a pushy friend with her (and even called her doctor's office myself at one point) until she got an earlier appointment, and she was able to be diagnosed and ultimately treated in a couple of days instead of having to wait a full week.

There are times when it is not us who has been dismissed, it is someone around us. This gives us an opportunity to stand up as an ally or an advocate and help make sure folks are not being dismissed. You read a little about how that might look in the previous scenario where I inserted myself on my friend's behalf to make sure she got an appointment and nudged her to make sure she was attentive to her health. Sometimes, though, we are trying to make sure someone we don't know quite as well isn't being dismissed. At times, being pushy like I was in the scenario involving my friend's doctor's office is inappropriate for the relationship. What follows are a few ways you can create an opportunity to make sure someone is not dismissed, but instead has their ideas included.

OPTION I

When you are the one speaking, invite the person who was dismissed to speak. This might sound like "I appreciate having the chance to speak, but first I am going to pass the mic to Ariel so she can speak more about her experience."

Why this works:

Folks might feel comfortable being dismissive of a single person, especially in a way that most people will not notice. However, whoever was being dismissive toward Ariel is unlikely to do it again when there is a third party involved.

OPTION II

Invite the dismissed person to be helped or supported ahead of you. This might sound like "I'm happy to wait until you finish helping the person who was here before me" or "I was after the person in the blue shirt."

Why this works:

This approach puts the individual offering the service or experience (or whatever it is) of having to deal with the dismissed person before they can move on to provide the service to you. This leaves the service person with the option of helping the dismissed person or skipping both of you, which is unlikely, especially if there are witnesses.

Tone and body language go a long way when it comes to stepping in as an ally for someone else. Keep your body language and tone very light and friendly when creating space for someone to get the assistance they need. While we may want to call the culprit out, it's helpful to remember that calling a person out explicitly is only helpful if it will result in a changed experience. Often, our role as an ally is to create opportunities for corrective action instead of creating a confrontation that ultimately does not solve the problem.

23

Medical Advocacy: When Feeling Intimidated, Dismissed, and Powerless Combine

I dedicate a specific section of this book to medical advocacy because it is one of the hardest spaces in which to speak up. Whether advocating for their own needs or the needs of their loved ones, folks can feel intimidated, dismissed, and powerless when speaking with physicians. While most of us trust our doctors and are always willing to hear their direction, sometimes doctors intimidate us because they know more than we do, even though we are living in our own bodies. Sometimes our doctors dismiss things we think are serious because they have the bias of dealing with medical concerns all day, and ours can seem minor. Sometimes doctors make us feel powerless because they ultimately determine the course of treatment for things that are happening to us, leaving us with the power of either abiding or finding another doctor altogether. Medical treatment is one of the greatest opportunities for inclusion in the world. There are all kinds of disparities in how people experience health, exacerbated by inclusion failures like limited access to care, racial bias, and lack of information. Speaking up when we are talking with our medical practitioners is one way we can begin to have more comprehensive health experiences. Inclusion in the case of our health care can literally be a life-or-death issue.

When we feel like our lives or health are on the line, it makes sense that speaking up would be a challenge. So while I give you language later in this chapter to help you speak up for yourself, I thought it was important to speak with someone who understands patient advocacy.

I spoke with Tamika Felder, founder of Cervivor, a global community of patient advocates who inspire and empower those affected by cervical cancer by educating and motivating them to use their voices for creating awareness to end stigma, influence decision and change, and end cervical cancer. In our conversation about speaking up, she shared, "One of the things that I share with patients is that if you can't speak up for yourself, you need to email the medical team. You need to write it down, take it with you, or have someone – a proxy or ally, whatever you want to call it – who will be there and can speak on your behalf. Let me just say, most doctors care, they want to save you, but there're also a lot of doctors who are talking at people versus making them a part of the process with something that has to do with them in their own bodies, so people can feel powerless."

Doctors are not always operating in their humanity; sometimes they are operating in their skillsets. They have read this or that research and determine a course of treatment based on what they have read. The reality is that many clinical trials do not include people who are from a myriad of racial and ethnic backgrounds, and people are different. But physicians can sometimes be really committed to what they know the research says over what their patient is saying. Additionally, myths such as that Black people can handle more pain may play a part in how physicians might treat. Patients end up not speaking up because, as Felder shares, "The truth is a lot of people feel like they are great at standing up for themselves, they're great at fighting, but there are a lot of people who are just taking the doctor, the expert, at their word, who says, you know, this is your standard treatment. Other times people have had past experience that tells them there is no reason for them to speak up because no one has heard them out in the past."

I am of the opinion that it is always worth it to speak up. Folks can't change their perspectives or behaviors if no one ever lets them know that what they are doing is wrong or not helpful. You can't hold anyone accountable for your treatment if you do not speak up. We tend to think that not speaking up affects only us and where we're currently at, which isn't true at all. Felder shares, "Using your voice isn't just about speaking up for yourself. It's also speaking up for others who are coming at a distance in the future, but even people who may see that doctor in the same week! So you really have to speak up and be heard and ensure that the conversation circles back to the doctor repeating back to you what you said, indicating understanding and ultimately being held accountable for your life."

People also think that speaking up has nothing to do with inclusion. The very first step of inclusion is sometimes acknowledging "there's something not right" and letting someone know about it. That might be in the ways that we're typically used to hearing about inclusion like in the workplace or getting service at a restaurant, but it is also in your day-to-day life, like when I'm getting medical treatment, because now your doctor is developing a habit with each encounter and that habit should include being inclusive of the patient's needs and ideas, to be a co-collaborator in their care. Medical advocacy is an inclusion matter as well. So when you speak up you are teaching your doctor to create space to think differently and be prepared to shift their behaviors to offer thoughtful and inclusive care. So even if you are not speaking up for yourself, remember, your speaking up can impact the system.

Tamika Felder experienced this firsthand. "When I was trying to preserve my fertility, one of the reasons why my insurance denied me is because I wasn't actively trying to conceive at the time of my diagnosis. I also wasn't married and because there's an archaic law in different states around the United States that if someone isn't married, they won't be covered for fertility services." Although she lost her fertility because of cervical cancer, she fought to have fertility preservation coverage enacted as a law in Maryland for future survivors of cervical cancer. "When you're looking at preserving fertility, you're looking at about $30,000 to $40,000 right out of the gate. Even if insurance is providing partial coverage, you still need $10,000 to $15,000. Most people don't have that. And you're also having to make this huge financial decision about your fertility, while you're also fighting for your life." The fertility preservation coverage that Tamika helped to get passed dictates that there is no way someone's fertility services can be denied based on anything, even if they're on birth control pills. Whether they're actively planning for a family or not and regardless of their gender, marital status, or any event, they can't be denied fertility coverage. Tamika will not benefit from the law, but because she has spoken up, many others behind her will.

There is a lot of bias in medical treatment. Earlier in this book, I mentioned the doctor's bias about Black men being opposed to surgery. But medical bias doesn't always work in the patient's favor. Tamika shared that there are many stories where a physician's bias will dictate what they will offer patients. She shares, "In medical care is the one place where you absolutely should not have a negative bias. But there will be patients who are asking for a specific hearing aid, and doctors will not offer it to them because they will assume they can't afford it because they are Black or Brown or whatever. The doctors didn't try to find any organizations to help pay for it, even though there are clearly organizations that can help. So what we're talking about isn't just survival. I think a lot of people look at the end game of survival, but people are not looking at how medical bias can impact the everyday quality of life."

Doctors are steeped in their knowledge and skillsets, but sometimes fail to consider that lived experience is still valid. They can dismiss a patient's personal experience in favor of what their research has taught them. Following is an example of pushing back against a doctor's recommendation that comes from my friend Amanda Miller Littlejohn, who wrote the Foreword for this book:

> *My son was hospitalized for asthma, so he started going to specialists. An allergist we went to put him on two medications, one of which is the strongest inhaler in its category. My son's mood changed – he went from a happy, easygoing kid to overtly hyper, disruptive, and emotional. I knew the medications were the only change. I brought it up to the doctor and he argued with me that the symptoms I was describing couldn't stem from the medications because those medications don't reach the bloodstream. He was very condescending and even tried to quote his own research paper because he's been recognized in his space as a super-expert on this. I know my kid. I also knew I could not compete with his knowledge. So, I pushed back by asking probing questions in a space I knew about, my child. "I appreciate that you know your research, thank you for sharing. Are you open to the possibility of trying another medication so I can monitor for behavior changes?" I asked. "Are you willing to consider that your research might not capture every scenario and try a less aggressive prescription in this case?" I pushed and pushed and got him to change the prescriptions, reluctantly. Sure enough, the symptoms went away.*

There are so many stories of people I know who did not push back against their doctors and they ended up suffering for it in the long run. What's really frustrating is that people often can sense that something isn't quite right. Our intuition kicks in, and we second-guess ourselves. It might be because we feel like we don't know enough or we don't have the power, or the doctor says that everything seems fine. Sometimes we are feeling anxious about creating inconvenience or work for someone else. Whatever the reason, we push that instinct aside. I have done it personally. Years ago I did not push back on a dentist who said I needed nine fillings when I had never had any before in my life. In my gut I knew it wasn't right. But I told myself, "Well, Amber, you don't know how to read X-rays," and I pushed my gut feeling aside. Here I am today with nine fillings I did not need because I did not speak up and say something as simple as, "That seems like a lot since my last X-rays a year ago. Is there another alternative to fillings at this time? Before I do that, I think I would like a second opinion."

There is a way to challenge doctors and other medical professionals and be assertive as well as respectful. In addition to the tactics presented in the preceding chapters on navigating how to speak up when you are feeling intimidated, dismissed, and powerless, consider using some of the following language to challenge experts in a medical setting.

OPTION I

"I understand that you do this for a living, so you have a lot of experience. I value that so much and that is why I am here. Are you willing to consider the possibility that I am having an experience that is a little different than what you have seen before? I would love the opportunity to explain it to you."

Why this works:

Folks who know a lot usually want to be recognized for it, but also sometimes need a gentle reminder that they may need to consider a different perspective. Acknowledging that you value their knowledge and want to potentially have them apply it differently will usually cause the expert to at least listen to hear what might be different (even if they think they have heard it all before) instead of being dismissive.

OPTION II

"Hmm. I understand that might be a typical approach, but I am not sure that will address my concern. I'd like to be a collaborator in figuring out the best course of action for my [child's/parent's/spouse's] health. Are you open to discussing solutions that might work better for my [child's/parent's/spouse's] body?"

Why this works:

This approach is great for inviting the expert to join you – in other words, to share their power – to get to a solution that works. Remember, framing your desires as a question rather than a directive invites people to give you an answer.

OPTION III

"I appreciate your expertise, thank you for explaining. Candidly, that doesn't quite sound right to me. Can I make a decision on that at a later time? I think I want to do some additional research and potentially get a second opinion."

Why this works:

You may not have the power to diagnose and treat yourself, but you do have the power to participate in your (or your loved one's) treatment. When you ask for time to research and share that you want to get a second opinion, it communicates that you are skeptical. Most physicians will lean in and try to answer any additional questions you have when they perceive skepticism. It's a great way to balance out the power in the interaction.

Remember, experts – especially doctors – are supposed to be helping, but because they are humans who often encounter the same things repeatedly, they slip into routines, too. Be prepared for the possibility that decorated experts might have a know-it-all energy and do not personalize it when they get defensive. The best way to disarm someone who is defensive (or who could be) is to turn up the curiosity and the warmth in your tone and turn down the snark.

24 Interrupted: What If I Keep Getting Talked Over?

Being interrupted is a really common workplace and general communication complaint. Although there is data that says both men and women interrupt one another, men tend to do more interrupting and have fewer social or psychological penalties for interrupting than women do, according to research from Joanna Wolfe, a teaching professor of English at Carnegie Mellon's Dietrich College of Humanities and Social Sciences.[1] While preparing for this book, dealing with interruptions was in the top five things people wanted to make sure I cover, so to be sure, interrupting is giving folks some serious grief.

How do you deal with being interrupted in the moment? I'm going to be honest, this one is tough. Many of us have visions of evoking Vice President Kamala Harris's "I'm speaking" with that one colleague who seems to always interrupt everyone, but we also worry about being seen as confrontational. Remember that nervy feeling I have described a few times in this book that can happen between our nose and our navel? Managing interruptions activates that feeling for me big time because there really isn't a way to avoid addressing the behavior being at least a little confrontational. Addressing an interruption always runs the risk of getting a little messy no matter how tactfully you address it. There just isn't a way to do it where you can be sure you won't potentially rub a leader the wrong way, although I have found addressing interruptions with confidence lands a lot better than addressing them in a pleading or nervous way. What should never be an option is letting interruptions go unaddressed, because that can encourage the behavior to continue.

---

[1] Jason Maderer, "Women Interrupted: A New Strategy for Male-Dominated Discussions," Carnegie Mellon University News, October 21, 2020, https://www.cmu.edu/news/stories/archives/2020/october/women-interrupted-debate.html.

Recognize that we can't move toward a more inclusive world by permitting the same behaviors that keep us excluded now, which means that even when there is a possibility that the discussion won't go perfectly smoothly, we have to commit to pushing past whatever bumpiness we are feeling between our nose and our navel and speak up. The following section offers a few techniques you can use to deal with interruptions.

OPTION I

When someone interrupts you while you are speaking, stop talking and look at them while they speak. When they finish their thought and you can detect that they are looking for a response from you, wait an additional couple of seconds, then kindly say, "Thanks for that perspective. I had something additional to share before you chimed in. Would you like for me to share my thoughts or would you like to change directions and discuss what you just said?"

Why this works:

This framing not only calls attention to the interruption, it also highlights to the culprit that they are missing information because they interrupted you. In most cases, folks will reply by asking you to share the rest of your thought before engaging on the next topic. On the off chance that they say they want to move on, do so. It might feel like they "won" – they didn't. Let it go and continue the discussion or ask to speak to someone else instead.

OPTION II

When someone interrupts you while you are speaking, continue speaking for a few moments as they are speaking – without raising your voice – and make friendly eye contact with them as you draw your sentence to a close. Likely the person will either stop talking and say "my apologies, please finish your thought," to which you can reply "thank you" and keep going. Alternatively, they may continue speaking and then will attempt to hand the conversation back to you, at which point you can reply, "Interruptions can cause people to lose their train of thought, so I'm not sure this is exactly what I was going to say, but I would like to add . . ." and continue your train of thought.

Why this works:

This approach causes the culprit to notice their behavior in the moment and have to either commit to it or back down from it. As most folks do not want to be seen as a person who interrupts others, both responses serve to force the culprit to acknowledge their behavior. The key to this approach is your confidence and body language. You can't shift into frustrated or angry energy even if that is what you are feeling. You should purposely position yourself with an inviting and professional posture as if to communicate, "I know you didn't intend to interrupt me, but let's make sure we don't make it a habit, friend."

OPTION III

When someone interrupts you, look at them and immediately state, "Just a moment, please let me finish my thought," and continue your sentence.

Why this works:

Executed quickly and confidently, the person who interrupted you will simply stop talking and let you finish because if they continue to speak it might feel like they are being confrontational. Most folks, especially in business exchanges, will avoid confrontation at all costs. In more casual spaces where people are more comfortable being challenging, this approach may be less effective.

Sometimes interruptions are best addressed as an ally. I notice I am very sensitive to how clients treat my team, and I tend to confidently lean in as an ally to stop inappropriate interruption. Here is an example.

I was in a client meeting supporting a team member who was driving the project. The meeting was a feedback meeting, which means I knew that emotions might run a little hot. My consultant (who is a Black woman) was talking to everyone about the pros and cons of sharing inclusion data publicly and the considerations to take into account to make the best decision on what data to share and when to share it. Mid-sentence, a junior member of the client's team (a Black man), who had made it clear earlier he felt the organization needed to be transparent with their data no matter what, jumped in to challenge my consultant in the middle of her sentence. I piped up loudly and immediately: "Excuse me, Roderick [not his real name], I believe Shae is still speaking about that." To which he replied, "I'm talking. Can I finish my sentence please?" "No, you cannot," I said pointedly. "Shae was speaking, and you cut her off. If you would like to be heard, you can wait until she finishes her thought." He got quiet. In fact, the whole virtual room did. I let the silence sit for a moment and then said, "Shae, I believe you had the floor." Shae said thank you and she continued on with sharing her thoughts.

After the meeting about six other attendees called me and said, "Oh my God, thank you! How did you do that? He cuts people off all the time and no one ever stops it!" Truthfully, I didn't even think twice about it. Roderick cut her off mid-sentence and I was not going to set the expectation that behavior like that would be tolerated by me or my team as we work toward helping this particular organization. This is allyship in action. Cabral Co. as a company has to role-model inclusion and equity, even when it is uncomfortable, so folks understand we are not just talking about this abstract concept, we are talking about impactful culture changes that take labor and a willingness to get uncomfortable.

But seriously, how did I do it? How can you speak up when someone is interrupting others? Following are two scripts to help you chime in and course-correct as an ally.

OPTION I

"My apologies, Casey, but you cut Amber off in the middle of her thought and I want to make sure I capture the full point. Amber, can you continue your thought, please?"

Why it works:

This approach does two things in one sentence: first, it stops the dialogue Casey started when they interrupted Amber. Second, it invites Amber to speak up without her having to be the source of whatever embarrassment Casey is feeling.

OPTION II

"Excuse me (pause here and look kindly at the speakers). Can we go back to what Amber was saying?" and look at Amber when you say that sentence.

Why this works:

In a fast-paced discussion, it is a short break in the flow that will usually silence the room and cause everyone to look for Amber to start speaking. This approach is good for senior leaders because it doesn't call them out directly in a meeting for interrupting, but it does role-model an inclusive approach to the discussion.

Be prepared for someone to try to continue speaking like Roderick did in the earlier example. You have to be prepared to hold your ground and tell someone no confidently, and perhaps use some of the techniques we covered in Chapter 16, Saying No While Still Protecting Your Reputation.

It is worth noting that as I was preparing content for this book, many women asked me what to do about men talking over them at work and in the household. So if you are a man – especially a cisgender, heterosexual man – there is a good chance you might be cutting folks off when you are talking to them, even if you do not realize it. There's no need to be defensive about it; remember, we all can sometimes engage in behaviors that we aren't aware of. The key is to be open to the possibility you are engaging in a noninclusive behavior and also be willing to shift the behavior. What follows are a few tips you can use to practice not interrupting people. These tips are great practice whether you are male or not, and even if you have not identified the behavior in yourself.

1. Wait a count of two full seconds after someone has stopped speaking to say something back. Yes, the two seconds will feel long.
2. When appropriate, jot down your thoughts so you don't lose track of them while waiting for your turn to speak. If it is a very serious conversation, taking notes can be seen as not paying attention. An option to overcome this is to ask something like, "I am taking

our discussion seriously, but I want to make sure I don't lose my own thoughts – do you mind if I take a few notes while we are chatting?" Make sure you are not writing rebuttals to what you are hearing – that isn't helpful. Focus on keeping up with your own thoughts only.

3. After someone wraps, you can ask, "Would you like for me to share my thoughts here?" Please don't be snarky with this ask. Instead, lean more toward using the kind of tone children use when they ask if they can stay the night with a friend or go see a new movie. "Can I go to the movies with Carmen, please?"

4. Listen to recordings of meetings and try to observe when you are interrupting others so you can be purposeful in those moments to hold your thoughts in future conversations.

Being interrupted is often demeaning to the recipient and can have the opposite effect of making someone feel valued, supported, and connected. It is worth taking some time to correct the behavior in yourself and knowing how to address it in others.

25 Framework: How to Speak Up and Advocate for Yourself and Others

Having the right words is one thing, but sometimes we just need to understand the best way to approach a difficult discussion. What follows is a high-level framework with an example to highlight the process of speaking up. Using this framework gives you the opportunity to choose your own language and approach, but still navigate speaking up with grace.

For a simple example, imagine you have put a deposit down on web design services, but the company is not meeting your expectations and is missing deadlines. You'd like to request a refund and find someone else to do the work. Start the conversation at level I of pushing back and speaking up.

1. **State your concerns with grace and empathy.** "I notice that you have not been keeping up with the schedule you committed to. I am concerned because the delays are impacting me in other areas of our planning. I understand that sometimes things happen that may impact our initial plans."
2. **Briefly recap the facts, including any actions you took to attempt to correct the issue.** "We have attempted to express our concerns with the schedule in meetings and have reached out several times to check in, but things still are not progressing in a timely fashion."
3. **State your desired outcome.** "Since you are not able to adhere to the schedule we agreed to, I would like a refund of my deposit so I can move forward with identifying another partner to execute the work."

Here is an actual email I sent from a scenario similar to our example:

> *Hi there [name redacted],*
>
> *It seems like your company isn't going to be able to deliver the work we agreed to on the two websites. Life happens, I hope things settle down soon. We were looking forward to the sites and I'm disappointed this didn't work out.*
>
> *My team member shared that she's contacted you a couple times but there's been no response. So I'm stepping in. We still have a deadline we'd like to make on these sites being completed.*
>
> *Can you please advise us on the process to receive our deposit back? Since you made the decision to not continue the work on schedule, it would seem to me a refund would be due.*
>
> *Looking forward to hearing from you!*
>
> *Amber*

Sometimes, a level I reaction is all it takes. The person you are working with might respond back by offering an apology and a refund or even more. This approach is straightforward, but also kind. It basically says, "Life happens, I hope things settle down soon. We were looking forward to the sites and I'm disappointed this didn't work out." Often when folks can perceive empathy, they are inclined to react positively and in your favor.

Occasionally, you will receive a reply that will require you to move on to a level II response, as I did in our web design example.

Here is the reply I received back:

> *Good morning Amber!*
>
> *Thank you for your patience in my response, and I thank you so much for your compassion.*
>
> *I completely understand your organization's need to move forward.*
>
> *Is it possible for us to come to an agreement on the refund amount for the initial deposit? We did not get to the design stage of the websites, but we did website planning for the Cabral company website, and I started the process of collecting content for the Cabral company website.*

*I'm happy to have a phone call or meeting with you and/or
your team about the deposit refund. I am happy to send the
amount that we agree to back electronically.*
    I look forward to your reply.
    ~[name redacted]

To be clear, there is nothing incorrect about this reply: it is respectful
and is a courteous attempt to negotiate. Unfortunately, a negotiation did
not feel like an equitable option for me in this scenario, so that means
I should move on to level II of pushing back and speaking up.

1. **Offer a summary of the related facts and restate your concern.** "I want to detail what I experienced so we can work from the same set of information. We agreed to a timeline on April 10, then ..." If you do not want to offend, try to avoid a bulleted list of events and instead stick to short paragraphs – bullets come across as being aggressive. Keep your tone precise, but not cold.
2. **Clarify the unseen.** Highlight information that may have been overlooked or not considered in the previous messages. "The impact of the project being delayed has cost us time and money by ..." Often folks don't consider how they have impacted you, so it is worth sharing if you make it to level II of a pushback discussion. Be clear about what you have experienced so the recipient has the full picture.
3. **Express empathy and request consideration for your circumstances.** "I can appreciate the work you have done, but I hope you are able to consider my experiences in your assessment of the circumstances." Just like in level I conversations, empathy can go a long way in keeping the discussion respectful and helps you role-model what it looks like to care and still have the desire to push back. Both can be felt.
4. **Address specific gaslighting, microaggressions, or diminishment of concerns if necessary.** If the person you are pushing back against has demonstrated gaslighting, microaggressions, or diminishment in their message, speak on it directly. "I notice your message said you executed work, but I want to make sure it is clear that we never received any executed work product."

5. **Restate your desired outcome.** "I think the appropriate next step would be to issue a full refund."

6. **Offer an opportunity for correction.** Even when we are recapping incidents, we might also miss something. It is courteous to offer an opportunity for the other party to share what you might have missed that could be relevant to the matter at hand. "Please let me know if I have missed anything or overlooked something in this summary. I want to be sure we are clear on all the details."

7. **Include any related parties on the message.** There are times when another party should be included on an email. For example, in the case of a refund, I may include someone in accounting or if a contract provision is in question, I will add my legal partner. There are times you may elect to copy your admin or your leader. Adding an additional party to an email also signals to the recipient that you are prepared to move toward a productive resolution where the copied parties will need to be involved.

Here was my level II response to the message above:

> Hi there, [name redacted]
> Let's be very forthright about this experience. We began speaking and a deposit was paid in the summer. Nothing went smoothly from there. While you mapped out the sites, and requested content – we also had several meetings to get the content outlined – you even had a meeting with my team (compounded time/$ wasted), have been nonresponsive to emails, and backed out on the timeline you created. I have repeatedly explained that my bandwidth is limited and yet I keep having to step in to move this forward – even now, to exit the agreement and request a refund.
> It feels like a gross diminishment of the facts to summarize the last several months as "we did website planning for the Cabral company website, and I started the process of collecting content for the Cabral company website."

While I can appreciate that you did something, candidly you've cost me time and money. It feels inequitable to not receive a full refund when none of the delays on this project were on my side and we did not receive any deliverables. There's also no way to get my sites done on the timeline I needed now as a result of your consistent delays.

I can empathize with life happening and I hope that whatever you're managing levels out soon. It's been a challenging year and as a company we've had to pivot as well. However, from a business perspective, a full refund makes sense in light of (a) you determined you can't keep the timeline you committed to, and (b) you have adversely impacted our deadlines to the point that we won't make them. We didn't change directions here, you did. It doesn't feel equitable to be financially responsible for that.

Unfortunately, I don't really have the bandwidth for a last-minute call – this also seems like a pretty clear-cut request where a call isn't necessary. I'm open to you sharing what I've missed here or if there is something in our agreement I haven't considered, but otherwise we've invested enough hours on unproductive dialogue. I'd honestly like a refund and to move forward in identifying someone else to execute the projects. Let me know how best to proceed.

Best,

A

In this example, the message is assertive and clear. It isn't rude, but it is setting the tone that there is no room to negotiate and what my expectations are. I copied my legal counsel because they handle all my legal matters, and I referenced our agreement with the company in the email. Lastly, my tone is indicative of the relationship – this person was a vendor for me. If I were emailing someone who held a superior position (perhaps where I was the vendor), my tone would be reflective of that relationship but still apply these seven steps. Here is an example of how the email may have shifted if I had been in the subordinate position.

Hi there, [name redacted]

I want to clearly recap our experience working together. We began speaking and a deposit was paid in the summer. Nothing went smoothly from there. While you mapped out the sites, and requested content – we also had several meetings to get the content outlined – you also had a 90-minute meeting with two other members of my team who are also managing other projects. We have struggled with your response time to our emails, and we have not received materials on the timeline you initially provided. This experience falls short of what we were expecting and is impacting our ability to deliver quality timely.

I understand that you did website planning for the Cabral company website and started the process of collecting content for the Cabral company website, but unfortunately those items were due in the first two weeks and are still incomplete. It feels inequitable to not receive a full refund when none of the delays on this project were on my side and we did not receive any deliverables. Additionally, the entire project timeline will need to be rescoped because of the delays.

I can empathize with life happening and I hope that things level out soon. It's been a challenging year and we've had to pivot as well. However, we still believe a full refund makes sense in light of the missed deadlines and the impact of the delays on the total project that were not in our control.

While I am unavailable for a call in the short term, if you can share some times that work for you to chat, I am sure we can also find time with my team, if not me. I'm also open to you sharing anything I've missed in this email. Lastly, I've also included our legal team in the event there is some relevant provision in the contract we signed that applies to this situation. I do hope you agree a refund is in order.

Let me know how best to proceed.

Best,

A

What you see above is the same message, but much less casual. The message is also framed to acknowledge that the sender, who also is the customer, is still more junior than the recipient. Remember, there is a way to say anything. You can say whatever needs to be said to anyone using this formula. Shift your tone and word choice to fit the dynamics of the relationship you are communicating within to be the most impactful.

These steps also work if the discussion is live and not over email. In person, you may not remember all the steps in the moment. That is okay. When I am in a conversation that could become a debate or otherwise tense, I don't necessarily recall these steps either. What I do instead is make sure that when I am feeling myself get frustrated, I remind myself that it isn't necessary. I also intentionally slow the pace of the discussion down so I can choose my words and my tone wisely. Don't rush, but don't shrink either. Remember, communication is what helps us get to results – it is almost always worth saying something when we are frustrated than to hold it in.

26 It's a Conversation, Not a Confrontation

onversations that give us nervous feelings, are about uncomfortable topics, or that require us to disagree are still conversations. Often those are some of the most important conversations to have! Whether we are getting or giving or giving tough feedback, it is still a conversation. We might not like how we feel in the moment, but remember that it is still just a conversation, not a confrontation. Confrontation is hostile and argumentative, and you should never have to reach that level of escalation using the techniques in this book. That doesn't mean you won't have feelings about a conversation where you and someone else are not seeing eye to eye. Let's explore some techniques to help you drive a confident conversation that holds people accountable.

Be Prepared

Before getting into a discussion that you know could be uncomfortable, make yourself some notes and outline your objectives for the discussion. Notes and objectives help to keep you on track and to not forget any of the points you want to say when you are in the meeting. It is especially helpful to have notes when you anticipate that you may be emotional about a meeting. Being prepared can keep us from losing the points we want to cover if we find ourselves affected by the discussion. Consider making yourself some light talking points or notes as a tactic to help you keep your composure in uncomfortable discussions and ensure that all of your concerns are addressed.

Invite Discourse

When we are concerned that a discussion may be challenging or uncomfortable, we might be tempted to skip it altogether. Inclusion and equity cannot happen without the necessary dialogue. Invite conversations that will be productive toward creating a culture of belonging, even if they start out a little rocky. When I think a discussion might be challenging, I lead with language around that to set expectations. For example, I might say, "This is challenging for me to talk about, but I think it is important for us to discuss to move forward." It might seem counterintuitive to share that you are feeling uncomfortable, but often you sharing that will disarm the person you are speaking with. Chances are, they are feeling uncomfortable too. Try not to see the dialogue as a problem, but instead see that it is a part of the process to get to an inclusive and equitable solution.

Share Your Opinion, without Challenging Someone Else's

I find it helpful to remind myself that I get to have my own perspective and so do others. We will encounter ideas that are not aligned with our own on all kinds of things. Politics, vaccines, holiday celebrations, and any and everything in between. Hearing different opinions helps us broaden our perspectives and learn to make space for other folks' ideas. The same is true for sharing our own opinions: they broaden others' perspectives and make room for more ideas. How you message your opinion, though, can help or be an impediment to that process.

When you share your opinion, just share it outright. Avoid transitional phrases like "I don't see it that way" or "I disagree with that" when you want to increase the likelihood of being heard. Instead, say something like "I appreciate you sharing that with me. My experience has been ..." This way you acknowledge what the person shared without diminishing it and then add your thought to the conversation. Very often more than one perspective can be true or valid so we can share ours and keep it if we would like while also creating an inclusive space for ideas that we do not align with.

Enroll Someone in Solving the Problem

I am a big fan of not taking on something that is not my responsibility or not entirely my responsibility. Very often, a problem is better solved with support instead of independently anyway! I do this by turning an "I" situation into a "we" situation. So instead of "I am upset that you didn't deliver my furniture on time!" I will say, "We can build a long-lasting consumer relationship if we can find a solution that gets my furniture delivered timely." Instead of "You gave up our reservation without even checking if anyone was here," I will say, "How can we get to a solution that gets my party seated with a reasonable wait time since it looks like our table was given away in error?" We, not I, is a subtle way to put accountability where it belongs. Someone raising their voice at you? Say, "We can get to a solution faster if we work to keep our tones and messaging respectful." Using a we approach when a problem is not solely your responsibility is a useful tactic to help move toward solutions and stay out of blame. It also acknowledges that you need assistance with getting to the solution since it is not your problem to solve.

Present Only Reasonable Options

When in an uncomfortable speak-up situation sometimes we will over-promise or over compromise to a fault to draw the conversation to a quicker close. Every single time we end up regretting the behavior because we don't end up with what we wanted, and it ends up costing us time or money. Stop presenting or even being open to options that do not meet your needs or standards. When we overpromise or over compromise, we end up using valuable energy; remember, inclusion means valuing yourself, too. What do I mean by present only options that are reasonable? Let's explore an example:

A company reached out to me about turning my first book, *Allies and Advocates*, into a series of videos. They wanted to pay me to do this, but the dollar figure was too low for the time commitment. I was uncomfortable saying no because of who the company is and the relationship they have with another company I work with. So, instead of declining outright, I attempted to negotiate a higher rate, and they wouldn't budge. I was set to decline the opportunity, but before I could do so, they offered to allow me to use the video content we create for my own company so long as I did not share it with any of their competitors. Ultimately, I agreed to do the work, so we signed an agreement and got to the process of scripting the videos.

Well, in the video scripting process, we realized that they had a very specific format they wanted videos in, and their format didn't work for my style of facilitation. I explained that I understood that they knew me as an author, but I am really a content developer and facilitator who wrote a book. I asked if they were willing to flex on the format and sent them a sample of me teaching. They emailed back, declining, stating the videos had to be the exact way they wanted them laid out – no flex. So, I declined the job. They reached back out, concerned that I was not going to do the work and shared how much time and money they had spent up to that point. They also offered to write the video scripts for me. I explained that the issue wasn't the scripts. The issue was the format of the videos. I needed to be able to facilitate in my style, not just because it was easier for me, but also because our agreement was that I would be able to use the videos. If the videos did not align to how I would actually teach the content, I wouldn't be able to use them.

Note that I didn't offer anything I wasn't willing to do, up to and including walking away from the job even after a contract was signed. The offer had to work for me and within reason or I had to walk away from doing the job. So I offered what was reasonable for me. We have to be very careful to protect our time and energy by not overcommitting our time or resources. We also have to speak up for what we actually want and need without losing sight of whether we are spreading ourselves too thin.

Ultimately, the company and I came to an agreement and I did the work they wanted, and they flexed the content in a way that worked well for me. It is always worth being clear with ourselves and others about what it is that we need and can do, even when we are under pressure to agree to things that may make someone else happy. Present options that are actual options.

Another way this shows up is when we are speaking with business partners or colleagues. You may find that someone you work with will frame something as your responsibility, even when it is not. That might sound like "How will you deliver on this project so we hit our goals?" when the responsibility doesn't rest with you to "deliver" but instead to "support." Pushing back might sound like "I am happy to support the project, but your role is delivery. My hope is that I can gain some insight on how to best partner to support so that we can hit your goals." If the option is not for you to deliver, respectfully make sure it is clear what the reasonable options are for you to support, not to deliver.

Take Advantage of Openings

Sometimes the discussion you are in will present openings for you to share your perspective and speak up for yourself or someone else. This can sound like someone sharing feedback with you, which can create an opening for you to also share your observations. The tricky thing with this is that feedback conversations can cause us to feel defensive or called out and we might miss the opportunity to push back appropriately. Here's an example from a client coaching where my client was speaking with a senior leader he supports. The leader said to him, "I am disappointed with how things have been going when we work with your team on bringing inclusion to life." He was immediately defensive, but because of our coaching, pushed that aside and instead said, "I'm so glad you brought that up! I have also been disappointed with our partnership. I would appreciate hearing your concerns and sharing a few of my own so we can get to some actionable solutions. Can we do that now?" The leader was surprised to hear that my client had concerns as well and she leaned into the discussion immediately. What my client did was take advantage of the opening. He heard through the "disappointment" to recognize that the leader wanted to talk. Since he had concerns as well, he took the chance to create an opportunity for the conversation to happen. Since the senior leader started by saying she was disappointed, my client was already prepared to hear some challenging feedback, so it did not derail the discussion. He also set her expectations in the moment that he too had concerns.

Openings take practice to spot. We are often so consumed with how we feel that they can be missed. Generally, I try to keep an ear out for them by paying attention to when someone wants to share some feedback – usually that means we can exchange feedback. I also recommend paying attention to your own fluctuations in temperament. If you catch yourself getting frustrated, it usually means you have something to share and should listen for an opportunity to calmly share it. Giving feedback, speaking up, and pushing back during openings does require you to keep your cool. Feel your feelings, but remember that you have something you want to get across, and consider your tone and word choice when you share it.

27 Keeping the Temperature Down in Tough Discussions

Sometimes we are going to speak up and it is going to set someone off. Next thing you know you have an angry person on your hands, and you are kicking yourself, saying, "I knew I should not have said anything!" Let's talk through what to do if you really upset someone.

First, don't beat yourself up. If you had good intentions and did not mean any harm, there is no reason to think, "I should not have said anything." There are several examples in this book and in everyday life of the kinds of bad behaviors that can go unchecked if people do not say anything. There will be times you will say the wrong thing! While your good intentions do not grant forgiveness, they should help you get to the point of apologizing for your mistakes pretty quickly.

If you set someone off and it is because you said something inappropriate, you should apologize. We covered apologies in Chapter 4, Feedback. But as a quick reminder, a meaningful apology sounds like "I apologize for _____. Moving forward I will _____." Sometimes you will need to say it more than once because when people are upset they do not hear you, and, because so few people really know how to apologize well, they likely don't expect a real apology. Keep your tone calm when you apologize; snarky apologies only irritate someone who is already upset. People may take some time to forgive you, but an apology sets things off in the right direction. It may take some time for you to earn someone's trust back, but that's normal. Think about how you respond when someone does something to hurt you. The apology is the first step. The next one is delivering on the "going forward" you committed to and repairing the relationship through your behavior.

What happens if you speak up about something and what you say is offensive to a whole room of people? Or you say something completely inappropriate online? The fact is, the first step is still the same:

meaningfully apologize. Most folks do not go viral for the foolish things they say on the internet. Those who tend to go viral have doubled down on their offensive or inappropriate message before apologizing. Those folks tend to end up experiencing all the negative backlash of an angry mob. My recommendation is to guard your online language and your public behaviors. If you say or do something inappropriate, you are more likely to feel bad or embarrassed than be a viral phenom. You also are less likely to be harassed if you sincerely and meaningfully apologize, quickly. By doing so, you immediately stop adding fuel to the fire, although you will still need to navigate the results of the initial behavior. As an added note, as a private citizen, you are less likely to go viral than someone who has some notoriety. This doesn't mean you shouldn't watch your behaviors; you should. But angst about being "canceled," as the young people say, is likely an unnecessary concern unless you are well-known or a celebrity.

Watch Out for Trigger Words and Statements

There are words that can trigger a big reaction from people, potentially even you, so be mindful of these words and how you use them. Trigger words can be unique to the individual, but there are some that are prone to get a rise out of a lot of people. Name calling (like "stupid" or "incompetent" or, these days, "anti-vaxxer"), as well as most -isms (racism, sexism, colorism, even capitalism) and phobias (transphobia, xenophobia, and homophobia as examples) can trigger angry and defensive responses, depending on the approach. Calling someone who is already upset racist, or sexist, can make for a bigger problem to manage. I am not of the opinion that attacking or shaming someone when they are upset is an effective approach, so I mind my word choice until I know I can be impactful. That said, I also believe in naming a thing a thing, so if something is racist or homophobic or whatever, using the correct words is appropriate. I just guard against attacking people with words I know are triggering; instead, I use my words as a tool to educate. Let me illustrate what I mean with an example.

Some years ago a client sent me their plans to review for their upcoming MLK Day celebration. As a part of the plan they were going to have the kitchen offer a lunch that consisted of fried chicken, greens, macaroni and cheese, and sweet potato pie. They were also going to offer a watermelon beverage to drink. My first thought was that this was horribly racist and deeply rooted in offensive stereotypes. However, if I said that to the team I was supporting, albeit true, it would immediately make everyone shut down, potentially missing the point. So, I contemplated my approach and decided that I would reserve my remarks on the plan for an upcoming meeting.

When the meeting day came, I joined the web meeting as planned. When the time came for me to share my feedback, instead of calling the menu racist, which I anticipated would cause everyone clam up, get defensive, and be embarrassed, I simply asked, "Can you help me understand why the menu includes fried chicken, greens, macaroni and cheese, and sweet potato pie on the date of the celebration?" Everyone was silent.

Someone spoke up and said, "Now that you say it aloud, it sounds bad, but I think we were looking at food as a part of the celebration of the life of Dr. King."

I replied, "What about Dr. King's legacy or the rest of the program connects to this menu selection?" Another long pause. I waited. No responses. I asked, "Do you understand why I am asking these questions?" A few confirmation nods, but no one said anything. When it became clear that no one was going to speak up, I said, "This menu appears to be rooted in racist stereotypes about what Black people eat. Unless there is a reason that this menu belongs with this program that I am missing, my recommendation would be that you change the meal plan. Perhaps MLK week is not the week for fried chicken and watermelon. Considering Dr. King's legacy and this misstep, I would appreciate some revisions to this plan that include some specific learning moments about race and racism for the upcoming MLK programming." The event was revised, without an MLK-specific menu, and was ultimately a success.

When you know you are going to have a discussion that potentially involves trigger words, plan what you want to say. Make sure the word you are using is the right word. For example, I have seen people call something racist when it was not racist at all. Joe Biden deciding that he is going to nominate a Black woman to the Supreme Court is not an act of racism; however, there are people calling the appointment racist because they mistakenly perceive anything mentioning race as being racism. Racism is a system of prejudice or discrimination against people of a certain race rooted in social and institutional power combined with racial privilege. Racism operates on the belief that the race with social and institutional power is superior. The recent Supreme Court appointment of Ketanji Brown Jackson is an attempt to balance the effects of social and institutional power that have resulted in there never being a Black woman appointed to the high court in the past. The appointment is actually an attempt at equity.

Adjust Your Formality to the Situation

In situations where folks feel uncomfortable, sometimes their defense mechanism is to be very formal. This can show up in conversation or even over email. A conversation that may have started out in a professionally casual tone that is suddenly very rigid and formal can also cause people to react defensively. Admittedly, I struggle with shifting to the formal myself when I am uncomfortable. What usually happens is the person I am talking to either stops talking or they will say, "Why are you being so formal with me?" If you catch yourself shifting to formal language because you are feeling uncomfortable or defensive, stop yourself and say, "I can get a little formal when I am feeling defensive. I'm going to work on adjusting my communication because I think this conversation is important." That statement lets the person you are speaking with know that you are aware of the change in the discussion and that you are working on it, which usually means people will give you a little grace.

As a general matter, keeping the temperature down in a tough discussion requires you to exercise your grace. You can't control what someone else will do, but making a point to approach tough discussions with grace and calmness can go a long way. In fact, our demeanor can cause someone else to adjust their demeanor. I have a personal example from just this week.

I received my COVID-19 booster over a month ago, but I did not get an update on my vaccine card when I went in. I think it was just a misstep on the part of the office. Well, recently a client was looking for me to share my vaccine status for an event and I realized I did not have record of the booster. I logged into the medical portal and there was no record of it there. I sent over a request for the information to be sent to me and received a message back that said, "We have no record of you getting a booster shot. Are you sure it was here?" I immediately panicked, double-checked my records, and upon verifying I was right about my visit, I got upset. What did they mean they had no record of my vaccine? What did they inject me with? How could I verify that I was boosted, and what lot number was it in the event something went wrong? I was both scared and angry as I headed into the medical center to talk to someone directly. As I approached the front desk, the woman behind it greeted me warmly, "Thanks for coming in. How can I help you?"

I replied, "I am really upset, so let me just set your expectations. I need to explain something to you, and I need it resolved immediately." She said okay, reached for a notepad, and listened as I explained everything to her. At the end she asked for my details to look me up and apologized profusely for what was happening to me. She was so nice that I couldn't be mad at her, even though I was so furious about the situation. She was calm, patient, and made sure to acknowledge that she understood everything as she was sorting it out. I ended up feeling comfortable enough to go home while she worked on it, and she called me with updates until it was resolved. The grace she gave me to be angry while also staying calm as she sorted the issue out made it so much easier to talk to her about what I needed. I can only imagine how much harder the entire experience would have been with someone who was frustrated with me while I was navigating the issue.

What If Someone Starts Yelling at Me?

When a discussion escalates to yelling or inappropriate tones of voice, you can very calmly say, "Can we mind our tones of voice in this conversation?" If the conversation continues to escalate, then remove yourself from the conversation by saying, "In my experience, yelling isn't an effective way to communicate. Let's take some time and come back to the discussion when we can speak in normal tones and listen to one another." The last thing you want to do is yell back. Get out of the situation immediately. Yelling might be a sign that a loss of self-control could be imminent, and being a part of that will not be useful for anyone.

What If I Want to End the Discussion?

You may speak up about something and get to a point in the dialogue where it either feels unproductive to continue or you realize that the point has been landed and you wish to discontinue the conversation. You can always, always exit a conversation with grace.

When you think a topic is unproductive to talk about, basically you can elect not to engage without being rude. I have a friend who is very passionate about her beliefs about where the coronavirus originated, and I have no interest in engaging with her on the dialogue for several reasons. When she starts in on a rant, I wait until the appropriate point and I very warmly say, "Thanks for sharing your perspective with me." And then I change the subject. She usually gets the hint. On the off chance she doesn't, and she attempts to invite me into conversation again on that subject, I will say very kindly, "My apologies, I wasn't clear. I have nothing valuable to add to this conversation. Can we change the subject?" That usually puts an end to the conversation without being mean or rude.

When you have been engaging in a conversation and you would like to end it, you can say in a courteous but firm tone, "Thanks for the dialogue, I appreciate hearing your perspective." Folks will usually get the hint that you don't want to discuss any further. If they continue to engage you can say, "I really appreciate your engagement and you sharing your point of view, but I don't have anything else to contribute to the dialogue." That approach will usually wrap up the conversation so you can move in a different direction.

Sometimes you don't have to say anything to end a discussion. I have found that being quiet and not feeding any dialogue to a discussion I do not want to take part in will cause people to change the subject on their own. When I choose to use silence, I watch my body language because I don't want to offend or communicate dismissiveness. I just don't have anything to say, so I don't say anything and that works perfectly fine.

What If I Speak Up and Nothing Changes?

Speaking up and pushing back can grant us a sense of immediate relief until we realize that the behavior change we were hoping for hasn't really happened. There are a few things to keep in mind about future changes so you can set your expectations. Some results aren't always immediate; it does take time for some shifts to take place. You can always observe and, where appropriate, gently remind people who you think are making a meaningful effort, but are still on the journey to shifting their mindset. This might look like correcting someone's pronunciation of your name or reminding them to role-model inclusive behaviors like meaningfully apologizing or being mindful of gender diversity. Adjustments like this can take some practice to get right and it is okay for you to grant some grace with the changes.

Other times, folks will publicly commit to shifting their behaviors and they won't actually do it. Revisit Chapter 8, Overcoming the Most Common Obstacles, under "Accountability," where I covered ways to hold people accountable for behaviors, especially when they have made commitments. Throughout this book, ways to hold folks accountable are given. Employ the techniques where possible. Remember, some folks just won't do things unless they are held accountable every single time. Others will flex with minor correction. People tend to resist change, so while it can be frustrating, try to anticipate the resistance so it doesn't burn you out and decide where it most makes sense to lean in and where it doesn't.

28 Any Questions?

I imagine the answer to that is yes. As I was writing this book, there were a number of things that came to mind or that people asked me when they reviewed early drafts of the book that felt important to include. This section is a compilation of answers to the most common questions I received and a few that I think are likely to come up after reading this book. If you have an unanswered question, it may be in this section. If you don't have any questions, this section of the book might still offer some useful ideas even if you haven't considered the questions yourself.

Amber, a lot of your framing seems to assume people have good intentions. What if I don't think they do?

As a general rule, I don't care what someone's intentions are, I care about results. So I work to communicate in a way that shows integrity and is also most likely to get me to the result that I want. Folks' intentions do not matter nearly as much as what they actually act on, so I elect to focus on folks' behaviors instead of their intent. This approach takes practice because we are conditioned to seek connection with people in conversations. I do that, too. When I notice we are not going to connect in a positive way, I stay focused on keeping a kind tone and demeanor and wrapping up the interaction as soon as possible – but not before any necessary business is handled.

How do I know when my company is finally inclusive?

There is no real goal post for inclusion because it is an evolving process. One doesn't achieve inclusion, but instead works to be inclusive in an ongoing way. There are a few things that are indicators of an inclusive culture:

1. People ask each other for constructive feedback and give it to one another.
2. Folks correct each other in the moment, whether it's name pronunciation (Christopher prefers Christopher, not Chris), inaccurate information, microaggressions, or any other opportunity to be inclusive.
3. Folks can disagree and still communicate with each other. No one feels the need to shut down even when folks are not able to see eye to eye.
4. People apologize without being asked to, and actively work to correct problematic behavior.
5. People try to find ways to learn about one another and respect each other's uniqueness.

Most importantly, folks understand that you will always be evolving. I know folks like to say that inclusion is a marathon, but it is really important to know that it is not a destination. It is an experience that you evolve to create as times and identities change. Look for ways to make it a part of your lifestyle instead of making it a checklist kind of goal. Also remember, sometimes it will be challenging to evolve; inclusion is not easy.

What if I am an introvert? How do I employ these techniques?

Being an introvert is about energy management. You like to concentrate and enjoy having time to process. You take your time making decisions. You are reflective and self-aware. Also, you may be quiet, preferring to speak only when necessary. You get energy from being alone and having time to yourself.

Being an introvert should not prevent you from employing any of the tools in this book. In fact, it is more likely that you will give things plenty of thought before you actually push back, which can be a great thing. Lean in and give some of the tactics a shot.

Sometimes people will say they don't speak up because they are an introvert, when introversion has little to do with that. I know some introverts who may not say much, but when they speak, everyone listens. It may be that you are shy or that you need to overcome one or more of the obstacles covered in this book, but simply being an introvert should not be what is in the way of speaking up.

A lot of the scenarios that you describe do not account for the possibility that I might be really upset or angry. How can I speak up when I am really angry about something?

The short answer? You can't. Take it from a girl who used to be the queen of matching other folks' energy, anger is almost never useful for a productive conversation. Wait until you are not too angry to talk. Walk. Find a relaxing activity. Chat with a friend or a therapist. I get mad, too, and when I'm mad I find it hard to address things, so I need to step away. When you calm down is when you should try to work toward a resolution, and it might be easier with a cooler temperament for you to find a technique in this book that could be useful for your unique circumstance. If someone is trying to press a conversation with you when you are angry, you can say, "I can appreciate that you want to talk about this, but I need to get my emotions together first."

A lot of these techniques seem like they would work well for communicating better in a romantic relationship. Do these tactics work in dating or relationships as well?

Yes and no. Let's put it this way – I am a very good communicator. A lot of folks I've dated were not as good at communication and could at times be intimidated in an intimate relationship with someone who they perceived

they "can never win an argument against," as one of my
exes so eloquently put it. I try very hard to make sure when
I am in a relationship that my partner understands me
and my unique style as well as understanding that I don't
need them to communicate the same way I do, but I do
need communication. I am also really good at apologizing,
because, after all, I teach folks how to apologize as a part
of my job. But factually, I am single and have been single
for a long while. Now that could be because I have some
personal preferences that could be obstacles or any other
environmental factors – like I live in Atlanta where the
heterosexual male-to-female ratios in the Black community
are very imbalanced. I'm not really sure. That said, you
can do with this information what you will, and I caution
you to use these techniques in your intimate spaces at
your own risk.

**This book and your previous book are focused a lot
on what individuals can do when a lot of times the
power rests with people who aren't willing to change.
Why do you take this approach?**

I think the work of being inclusive and equitable is
work that has to be approached from many different directions, addressing the structures like organizations and
government entities and policy as well as getting individuals' support. While I don't do all the things, in my
consulting practice at Cabral Co. we work with corporations and their leaders to move this work forward in organizations and government entities. I also think getting
resources to the people individually is important, because
although not all people have the kind of power to change
organizations and government policies, all of us can
change ourselves. And there are a couple of magical things
about that. Organizations are made up of people. Govern-
ments are made up of people. People are the consumers.
People are the manufacturers. People grow the food. People
run the restaurants. This entire system is in service of and
powered by people. Also, people imitate each other.

We adopt each others' habits and ideas and styles of communication. So if enough of us are working to be inclusive, working to speak up, working to create equitable spaces, and enough folks imitate each other, this whole thing can start to shift.

I don't anticipate overnight change. I do believe that for however much the negative is imitated, duplicated, and communicated, it is worth it to put a little positive in the system and see how folks do with that. Because in a way, some of the power actually does rest with the people, but so many of us are too scared to try anything different.

You covered a lot of scenarios in this book, but I didn't see one about what to do if someone is just plain lying to you. Can you offer some language for that?

There were so many different things I wanted to add to this book, and lying is a really big one. Lying is also hard to cover because how you should navigate lies depends so much on how the lie is happening. Is it behind your back? Is it in front of others? Is it about your work contributions? Is it in a team environment? In lieu of a chapter, here are a couple of small techniques to use when someone is lying that might get them to stop or expose them. If the lie is in front of you, you can say, "That is not how I recall things happening; can you share more detail so I can get clear on where the disconnect is? I want to make sure I understand since I am involved." Make the person lying share more. Liars get caught when they have to give the details.

Another option is to challenge the lying person with facts in a curious way, like "I think you are saying I did not contribute to this project, but this table you constructed is leveraging the data I shared. Maybe I am confused: Can you share what you mean by contribute? I may be misunderstanding." If a lie is happening behind your back, I recommend casually inviting the person to share it in mixed company by bringing the topic up so they have to expose themselves. Angrily confronting a liar can make you look like the bad guy; instead, you want to strategically invite them to tell on themselves.

The following are a few other scenarios I didn't get to dig into in this book, but that I think it might be helpful to have language for:

- If someone is trying to convince you to do something or attend something you don't want to participate in.

  Say: "I appreciate you sharing the options with me. I'm satisfied with my choice to not attend/participate."

  If they press, you can say, "I appreciate you are excited! I hope it turns out as good as it sounds and (only if you mean it) I am looking forward to hearing about it."

- If someone has done something wrong or inappropriate and attempts to gloss over or dismiss it as no big deal.

  Say: "We moved on pretty quickly and sometimes things get missed that way. I would like to revisit something that happened earlier to ensure you understand the impact of your actions." Then share your concern.

  If the person cuts you off while you are sharing, don't allow them to take the conversation over. Quickly say, "Just a moment, I know you want to share, but please allow me to finish," and continue your thought. After you are done sharing your concern, you can say, "Thanks for listening. I think it will make us more effective going forward."

- If you are feeling taken advantage of, you can say, "Pardon me if I misled you about my flexibility, but this opportunity sounds like more than I'm able to support. What I'm able to do is . . ." Then use the next few sentences to reset the person's expectations. It helps if you end with a question like, "Does that sound like something you'd be interested in?" or "Is there an opportunity for us to make this work keeping this in mind?"

  This works whether it is about someone taking advantage of time, money, or a certain skill; just change "flexibility" to whatever it is the person is trying to get from you unfairly.

- If you need to have a tough conversation with someone you love and care about, you can use whatever technique applies in this book, but open the dialogue with vulnerability. Vulnerability is a powerful connection tool. Use an opening phrase that messages your care like:

- "This is challenging for me to share because I love you, but it's important for me to be transparent . . ."
- "I'm really nervous about discussing this because I care about you, but it's important that I do."
- "I'm worried about how to have this discussion because I don't want to hurt your feelings/disappoint you/overwhelm you/ and so forth."

- If someone is trying to make you feel responsible for something you are not responsible for, you can push back by clarifying ownership or clarifying the flow of information. For example, "I understood the process was that you would notify me if I had a delivery. Am I misunderstanding?" Now the person has to clarify the process and their role in it, which allows you to hold them accountable.

  Another option would be "It sounds like this process did not take my circumstances into consideration. How would you suggest we get to a solution that works for everyone?" Now the person has to admit that they need to adjust and figure out how they will do that. Essentially you want to responsibly message "I don't own this, but you do" and help the person you are engaging with to come to that realization. I recommend that you use your curious tone of voice for circumstances when you are pushing back on someone who is trying to pass ownership off to you.

  Lastly, you can always say, using your curiosity, "Can you help me see how this is my responsibility?"

I realize that it is still possible that you will have a scenario that isn't covered in this book at all, but many of the tactics here work for a myriad of circumstances. Ideally, even if you cannot find your exact circumstance presented, you should still find language that will work for you.

29 Be Good to Yourself

The work of equity is eventful, evolving, and impactful, and the work of making space for the uniqueness of others, committing to use your voice when it is needed, and advocating for your own identity is playing the long game. Many of the liberties my ancestors dreamed of, they never saw. Many of the ones I dream about, I will never see. Seeing, though, isn't really the goal. The real goal is to make a meaningful and enduring impact. That means we have to recognize that inclusion and equity will not be solved tomorrow and potentially, in some ways, not in our lifetimes. We do get to get the ball rolling, though.

With that said, though, it is easy to want to give up or even to feel burned out. My dear friend José Vilson (executive director of edu-color.com) always tells me when we depart one another's company, or even when we end a phone call, "Be good to yourself." In the years since I've become a full-time small business owner teaching inclusion and equity to some of the world's most well-recognized brands, as well as students and nonprofits, those words have become increasingly important. So in closing this book, I share his words with you: be good to yourself. You are learning. Continue to. You will make mistakes. Learn from them. You are making an impact. Be good to yourself.

My hope is this book has given you some foundational diversity, equity and inclusion learning, an understanding of the many ways identity can shape how we show up, and, most importantly, the will to push past whatever obstacles you encounter so you can make an impact. There are a lot of scripts and tactics that you can make your own so you have the language to confidently communicate when things are not quite right for you or for others. I know speaking up and pushing back are not easy, and I know this book doesn't remove all doubts or uneasiness about what can go wrong when we advocate for ourselves and people we care about. But by applying the techniques and resources in this book, ideally you feel more prepared and therefore more willing to speak up even in the absence of ease. We need you for the long game.

Go forth and be brave.

About
the Author

Amber Cabral is an author and inclusion and equity strategist focused on helping organizations of various sizes and across industries to create and execute strategies to achieve sustainable leadership and inclusion objectives. She is the founder and principal consultant at Cabral Co., where her work has touched thousands of people, including Fortune 500 executives and senior leaders at multibillion-dollar global organizations, worldwide. Amber is best known for delivering respectful, authentic, and no-nonsense training, strategies, and content that is rich with simple but impactful steps and eye-opening insights that inspire change.

Formerly a senior strategist on the Global Culture, Diversity, and Inclusion team at Walmart Stores, Inc., Amber has experience with developing and executing strategies to achieve transformational culture change, embed diversity objectives, and inclusive behaviors into the employee lifecycle to ensure business relevance and representation. During her tenure with Walmart, Amber also served as a leader in Global Talent Management, where she designed and launched several organizational development programs, revamped the Mentor Me program, expanded the Corporate Intern experience, and created achieve, attraction, and retention objectives.

Prior to her time at Walmart, Amber spent eight years in health insurance in service and support roles of progressive responsibility. During her career at Blue Care Network of Michigan, she was appointed as a lead for corporate diversity and inclusion initiatives and was recognized for supporting the creation and launch of company-wide diversity training. She also gained experience in developing targeted marketing tactics and stimulating business growth through advertising.

Amber completed her thesis research project on andragogy (adult learning theory) to achieve a master's in organizational leadership and management from Siena Heights University in Adrian, Michigan. She also holds a bachelor's degree in psychology with a minor in sociology from Wayne State University in Detroit, Michigan.

Amber's passion for culture and people development extends beyond her professional role. She serves as the board chair of Brown Girls Do™, best known for its ballet arm, Brown Girls Do Ballet™, an organization committed to promoting diversity in the arts by providing annual scholarships, a mentor network, dancer resources, and community programs to empower young women and girls.

Originally from Detroit, Michigan, Amber currently resides in Atlanta, Georgia. She is visibly passionate about the value of improving representation, education, access, and opportunity for underrepresented people. This is her second book. She completed her first book, *Allies and Advocates*, published by Wiley in 2020. In her free time, she writes articles focused on race, culture, and working-class life; hosts a podcast called *You Can Have Whatever You Want*; consumes copious hours of audiobooks; and loves to travel.

Index

A

Ableist, term (impact), 67–68
Access/treatment, ensuring, 96
Accolades (reward), 81
Accountability, 181
  culture, cultivation, 22
  obstacle, 39, 42–47
  questions, 44
  request, 77–78
Advocacy, 31, 85, 161
  allyship, contrast, 28
  performative allyship/advocacy, 81
Allies and Advocates (Cabral), 1, 9, 15, 20,
  32, 52, 171
Allies, relationship (building), 52
Ally
  role, 157–158
  service/role, 142
  tone/body language, usage, 146
Allyship, 31, 85
  advocacy, contrast, 28
  attempt, 86
  opportunity, 130
  performative allyship/advocacy, 81
American culture, trauma
  (relationship), 57–61
Anger, control, 185
Apologies, 175, 180, 184
  preparation, 21–22
  teaching, 186
  usage, 131
Ask, declining, 116
Askers, accountability, 114–115

Associates, power imbalance, 124–126
Awareness, creation, 148

B

Bandwidth, absence, 165
Behaviors
  addressing, 69–70
  change, accountability, 72
  classification, 86–87
  denial, 111
  focus, 183
  inappropriateness, 132
    acknowledgment, 136–137
    addressing, 135–136
  intentional behaviors, 55
  microaggressions, 127–128
  performative behavior, assessment, 81
  public behaviors, guarding, 176
  shift, 45
  warmth, 140, 141
Belonging, sense (creation), 36
Bias, 4, 15
  doctor, bias, 16
  identification, 17
  problems, 16
  understanding, 17
Biden, Joe, 177
Binary thinking, 41–42
Black, Indigenous, and People of
  Color (BIPOC), 8
Black Lives Matter, 53, 87
Blatant disrespect, 135–138
Board/executive team diversity, 84

Body language, 70–75, 105
  communication, 65
  impact, 146
  open body language, usage, 140
  tactic, selection, 75
  tone, matching, 72
Boundaries, 91–94, 101
  defining, 109
  exercise, 104
  firmness, 103–104
Brown Girls Do Ballet™, 56
Burnout, 76–79
  source, 76–77, 79

C

Cancel culture, 50–51
Candor
  culture, cultivation, 22
  importance, 9
Capacity, focus, 102
Career goals, stretch assignment
    (alignment), 105
Centering, 11–12
Change, 94
  accountability, 72
  chance, 95
Chauvin, Derrick, 53
Children, store associate (power
    imbalance), 123–124
Civil Rights Movement, 53–54
Code-switching, 61
Collaborator, role, 152k
Comfort, prioritization, 54–55
Communication
  adjustment, 178
  habits/ideas/styles, adoption, 187
  misstepping, 54
  process, 70–71
  questions, 66
  style, ineffectiveness, 136
  techniques, adaptation, 185–186
  tools, 65
Communities, engagement, 136
Community investment dollars,
    diversification, 84
Company
  diversity/inclusion, 83
  values
    expectations, alignment, 137
    inclusion, relationship, 43

Concerns
  diminishment, addressing, 163
  stating, 161, 163
Confidence
  finding, 76
  projection, expectation, 135–136
Confrontation, conversation (contrast), 169
Connecting
  behavior, activation, 10–11
  role, 12
Constructive feedback, request, 20–21, 184
Contributions, acknowledgment
    (absence), 94
Conversation
  cessation, desire, 180
  confrontation, contrast, 169
  engagement, 180
  Level I pushback/speaking up, 161–162
  obstacles, 92–94
  opportunities, 173
  re-invitation, 180
  vulnerability dialogue, 188–189
Cooper, Edith, 128
Corporate giving, diversification, 84
Correction, 181, 184
  opportunity, offering, 164
CROWN Act, 131
Culture
  fit, 57
  understanding, absence, 35
Cultures
  shaping, speaking up (impact), 95–96
Curiosity, impact, 72

D

Dating, communication
    techniques, 185–186
Deaf ears, 66–68
Defense mechanism, formality, 178
Defensiveness, avoidance, 21
Differently-abled, term (usage), 86
Directives, usage, 103
Disabled, term (avoidance), 85–86
Disagreement, communication
    (continuation), 184
Discomfort
  obstacle, 39, 53–55
  occurrence, 54
Disconnect, noticing, 145
Discourse, invitation, 170

Discrimination, discussion, 53–54
Discussion
  cessation, desire, 180
  preparation, 169
  temperature control, 175
Dismissed person, assistance/support, 146
Dismissiveness, 143
  comfort, 146
  feelings, 143–144, 147
  scenario, 145
Disrespect, 135–138
Diverse vendors/partners, location
    (difficulty), 84
Diversity
  leader, 7–8
  trainings, usage, 131
Diversity, equity, and inclusion (DE&I), 8
  initiatives, 113
  language, knowledge, 1
  leading (voluntolding), 83–84
  learning, 191–192
Diversity, equity, and inclusion and
    bias (DEIB), 8
Doctors
  bias, 16, 149–150
  humanity, 148
  lived experience, validation failure, 150
  pushback, 150–151
  routines, 153

E
Ego, reduction, 66
Embarrassment, impact, 67–68
Emotion, expression, 74
Empathy, 28
  development, 27
  perception, 162
  usage/expression, 161, 163
Employee/employer relationships, power
    dynamics, 62
Employee survey, boundary
    example, 101–102
Energy
  management, 184–185
  usage, 72–73
Engagement, 86–87
  commitments, 91–92
Equity, 33, 42–43. See also Diversity, equity,
    and inclusion
  assigning, 83

charity, comparison, 34
conversation, 76–77
details, 36
experiencing, 13
expertise, 83
impact, 83
inclusion and equity Olympics,
    avoidance, 85–87
racial equity, 76, 77
success, 114
Experience
  influence, 68
  personal experiences, impact, 83
  recap, 166
  value, 151–152
Expertise, functional area (delineation),
    114
Experts, speaking up, 117
Explanations, appreciation, 120
Eye contact, 156

F
Facilitation style (adjustment), monotone
    voice (usage), 71
Facts, summary (offering), 163–165
Fatigue, 76–79
Favorability power dynamics, 62
Fear, 94
  obstacle, 39, 47–51
  questions, 48–49
  resonance, 51
  speaking up, fear, 141–142
Feedback, 8, 19, 63, 175
  advantage, 19–20
  apologies, preparation, 21–22
  appreciation, 21
  appropriateness, 24
  constructiveness/usefulness, 20–21, 184
  conversations, issues, 173
  defensiveness, avoidance, 21
  inviting, 21
  receiving, 54
  seeking/expecting, 20–22
  sharing, 23, 77, 174
  speaking/giving, 22–24
Felder, Tamika, 148–150
Fertility (preservation), insurance
    (denial), 149
Floyd, George (murder), 48, 53, 76–77
Focal point, clarity, 111

Follow-up conversations, usage, 142
Forgiveness, 175
Formality, adjustment, 178–179
Framework, 161
Framing, assumptions, 183
Frustration
  creation, 132–133
  sense, 144
Functional skills, boundary, 104

G
Gaslighter
  amazing/abusive cycle, operation, 112
  negotiation, 112
  one-on-one interaction, avoidance, 111
  positive reinforcement, impact,
    111–112
Gaslighting
  addressing, 163
  control, 111
Gender
  options, 36
  removal, 8
Glass ceilings, breakage, 79
Global pandemic, fallout (navigation), 53
Goals, 77
  career goals, stretch assignment
    (alignment), 105
  focus, 101, 102
  leader goal, example, 104–105
Grace, usage, 161
Growth mindset, 5, 8
Guilt, impact, 116

H
Harris, Kamala, 155
Health experiences, comprehensiveness,
  147
Hearing
  importance, 91
  obstacle, 92
High-level framework, 161
Home/friends, speaking up, 117
Homophobic language, change, 11
Humor, usage, 72–74

I
Ideas/contributions, acknowledgment
  importance, 91–92
  obstacle, 93

Identifier, tokenization, 52
Identity, 74
  complexity, 4
  evolution, 4, 8
  interactions, navigation, 3–4
  pronouns, relationship, 6
  sharing, 3
  trauma, 61
Ike, Ifeoma, 35, 51
Imitation, 186–187
Inappropriateness
  attention, 188
  identification, 23
Inclusion, 42–43. *See also* Diversity, equity,
    and inclusion
  achievement, absence, 13
  adoption, 43–44
  assigning, 82, 83
  behaviors, activation, 10
  bringing, 45
  conversation, 76–77
  defining, 7
  evolution, 12
  expertise, 83
    absence, 108
  failures, exacerbation, 147
  go-to techniques, 78
  impact, 83
    minimum, 46
  occurrence, 36
  performative inclusion, 85
  prerequisite, 41
  prioritization, 46
  success, 114
  time, 55
  training, 131
  usage, 10–13
Inclusion and equity Olympics, avoidance,
    85–87
Inclusion, diversity, and equity in
    action (IDEA), 8
Inclusive communication, example
    (sharing), 45
Inclusive cultures, building, 79
Inclusive experience, focus, 132
Inclusiveness
  commitment, 45
  knowledge, 184
Inequitable behaviors, 68

Information
  absence, 147
  inaccuracy, 184
Information/resources access
  importance, 92
  obstacle, 94
Insurance, denial, 149
Intentions, impact, 183
Interruption
  addressing, messiness, 155–156
  ally, role, 157–158
  apologies, 120
  behavior, acknowledgment, 157
  cessation, technique, 158–159
  framing, 156
  problem, 155
  reactions, 156–157
Interview, process, 32
Intimidation, 49, 119, 121
  feeling, 147
Intimidator
  accountability, 121–122
  subject matter, understanding, 122
Introvert, techniques, 184–185
Isms, impact, 176
"I Won't Be the Last" (Ike), 35

K
Knowledge, intimidation, 121

L
Language, 99
  tools, leverage, 75
  usage, 188
Leaders
  accountability questions, 44
  behavior, change (accountability), 72
  business partnership, assignment,
       107–108
  discussion, pressure, 108
  expectation, 137
  goal, example, 104–105
  professional mask, dropping, 46
Leaning in, 103
Learning
  continuation, 191
  journey, 78
  willingness, 5
Level I/Level II responses, 162–165
LGBTQIA+ communities, silence/
    blending, 58

Listening, absence, 144
Lying, reaction/challenge, 187–188

M
Medical advocacy, 147
Medical treatment, bias, 149–150
Mehrabian, Albert, 70
Men, talking over others
       (reactions), 159–160
Mental muscle, reprogramming, 133
Message (messaging)
  confidence, 76
  delivery, 100
  emotional impact, 70, 71
  five-question technique, 70
  focus, example, 102–103
  framing, 166–167
  impact, 66
  nonverbal elements, 70
  offensiveness, 69
  recipient, 68–69
  repetition, 120–121
Microaggressions, 127, 184
  addressing, 163
  avoidance, 128
  behavior, ally (impact), 131–132
  clarity, request, 129
  impact, 127–128
  minimization, 130
  occurrence, 134
  responses, 129
  speaking up, avoidance (impact), 128
Miller Littlejohn, Amanda, 150
Mindfulness, 55
Misgendering, 132–134
Misinformation, countering, 1
Mission, 44
Missteps, occurrence, 21
Mistakes, making, 91
Mistreatment, 41, 135
  avoidance, 63
Moxley, Reisha, 59–60, 62–63

N
Name calling, impact, 176
Names, 4–6
  correction, 184
  pronunciation, problem, 124–126
Negative backlash, 176
Negative bias, absence, 150

Negotiation, 112
Neurodivergent encounter, 88–89
Nonbinary pronouns, usage, 133
Noninclusive behavior, 68
  engagement, 159
No, word (usage), 113
  formula, 115–116
  techniques, 114–115

O

Obstacles
  overcoming, 9, 94, 139, 142, 181
  types, 39
Offerings, reasonableness, 172
Online language, guarding, 176
Open body language, usage, 140
Openings, identification, 173–174
Opinion, sharing, 170
Opportunities, exclusion, 41
Oppression
  discussions, 53–54
    increase, 12–13
  experience, 88
  overcoming, 79
  uniqueness, 88
Oppression Olympics, avoidance,
    87–89
Options
  presentation, 171–173
  sharing, 188
Organization
  goal, 45
  leader, impact, 82–83
  performative aspects, 81–85
Outcome, statement/restatement,
    161, 164
Ownership, avoidance, 101

P

Parent/child power dynamics, 62
Participation (avoidance), language
    (usage), 188
Partnering, confusion, 108–109
Peer pressure, 116
People
  assumptions, 4
  centering, 11–12
  identity, 3–4
  LGBTQIA+, 50

mistreatment, 41
  avoidance, 63
  model, setting, 100
  naming, 4
  perception, 50
  silencing, fear (impact), 47
  speaking up, fear, 50
People-pleasing
  avoidance, 107
  disadvantages, 109–110
Performative allyship/advocacy,
    81, 113
Performative behavior, assessment, 81
Performative inclusion, 85
Performative organizations,
    81–85
Personal experiences, impact, 83
Personal/familial trauma, 60–61
Personal life, boundaries, 103–104
Personal matters, example, 34–35
Personal routine, 55–56
Perspective, sharing, 173
Physical/psychological safety, 12
Physician treatment, myths, 148
Police brutality, protests, 87
Post-traumatic stress disorder
    (PTSD), 60–61
Power
  ability, 27
  absence, 62
  approach, 186–187
  awareness/usage, 23–24
  dynamics, 61–63
    examples, 62
  imbalance, 123
  usage, 96
Powerlessness, feeling, 147
Privilege, 19, 25
  awareness, 23–24, 28
  checking, 28–29
  consideration, 26
  existence, 26–27
  extension, 27
  negative perceptions/associations, 25
  problem, 27
  usage, 23–24, 28, 96
Problem solving, others
    (enrollment), 171
Promotion, assistance, 101

Pronouns
  misidentification, pushback/speaking
      up, 133–134
  practice, 5
  they/them pronouns, usage, 17
  usage, 4–6
      avoidance, 17
Pronunciation, accountability, 126
Public acceptance (reward), 81
Public behaviors, guarding, 176
Punctuality, importance, 99
Pushback, 91, 133–134, 161
  benefits, 95–97
  change, absence (reaction),
      180–181
  difficulty, 57
  minimization, 127–128

Q
Queer, term (usage), 8
Questioning, answer clarity
  importance, 91
  obstacle, 92–93
Questions, 183
  answer, request, 130
  asking, 105–106, 120
  response, requirement, 140
  usage, 116

R
Racial equity, 76, 77
Racial/racist stereotypes, 57, 176–177
Racism
  discussion, 53–54
  system, 178
Recharging, plan, 79
Recipient, response (expectation),
      68–69
Recommendation, usage,
      121–122
Reflective behavior, 184
Relationship
  building, 52–53
  communication techniques,
      usage, 185–186
  repair, 175–176
Repetition, usage, 120–121
Representation, 47
  underrepresentation, 49, 139

Reputation
  damage
      avoidance, 136
      fear, 47
  destruction, avoidance, 108
  protection/securing, 113
Resentment, avoidance, 107
Resolution, aim, 103
Resources, supply, 186
Respect, 55, 184
  disrespect, 135–138
  importance, 91
  obstacle, 92
  showing, 132
Response, expectation, 69
Responsibility, language (usage), 189
Retaliation, fear, 50–51
Role, clarity, 110
Role-modeling, 110
  sharing, 44
  treatment, 100

S
Self-advocacy, 161
Self-awareness, 140, 184–185
Self-care, 191
Self-diagnosis/self-treatment,
      power (absence), 152
Self-protection, 59
Self-treatment, 100
Senior leaders, meeting, 67–68
Sentiments, 43
Shared beliefs, impact, 41
Shared connection/interest,
      115–116
Sharing, appreciation, 144, 150
Silence
  expectation, 59
  safety, comparison, 48
  value, 94–95
Skillset, expansion, 5
Social distancing, 141
Societal power dynamics, 62
Space, safety, 51
Speaker
  appreciation, 120
  perception, 119
Speaking, dismissiveness, 146

Speaking up, 117, 133–134, 161, 173, 180
  anger, control, 185
  application, 116
  avoidance, impact, 128
  benefits, 95–97
  example, 124–125
  expectation, 135–136
  fear, 141–142
  impact, 175
    absence, reaction, 180–181
  obstacle, 119
  techniques, 108–109
Speak-up situation, options
    (presentation), 171–173
Statement, offensiveness, 130
Stereotypes, 140
  countering, 50
  racial stereotypes, 58
  referencing, 3
  reinforcement, 128
StopAsianHate, 87
Store associate, children (power
    imbalance), 123–124
Strangers, engagement, 94
Strategic questions, asking, 45
Stretch assignment, 101
  career goals, alignment, 105
Subject matter, understanding, 122
Supporting
  behavior, activation, 10–11
  role, 12
Systemic/systematic racism, discussion
    (increase), 12–13

T
Taking advantage, reaction, 188
Talent, diversity, 84
Team
  leader, expectation, 137
  player, perception, 139
  success, commitment, 141–142
Temperament, adjustment, 10
Threat, 49
Time (obstacle), 39, 55–56
Tokenism, 52–53
Tone, 70–75, 105
  body language, matching, 72
  communication, 65
  impact, 146

  setting, 115
  tactic, 75
Transitional phrases, avoidance, 170
Trauma
  American culture, relationship,
    57–58
  impact, 76
  occurrence, 59–60
  personal/familial trauma, 60–61
Treatment
  mistreatment, 41, 63, 135
  unfairness, 139
Trigger words/statements,
    avoidance, 176–178
Trust, building, 19

U
Unconscious bias, 15
Underrepresentation, 49, 139
Understanding
  obstacle, 39–41
  phrases/sentences, usage, 40
Uniqueness, respect, 184
Unseen, clarification, 163

V
Vaccinations, handling,
    178–179
Values, 44
Valuing
  behavior, activation, 10–11
  role, 12
Video scripting process, 172
Vilson, José, 191
Vision, 44
Voice, usage, 148–149
Vulnerability
  dialogue, 188–189
  knowledge, 75
  usage, 72–74

W
Whiteness, perspective, 59
White person, management (example),
    60
White supremacy
  culture, 59
  discussions, increase, 12–13
Wolfe, Joanna, 155

Word choice/approach, 65–70
  environment, impact, 66–67
  usage, 71
Words
  racist history, 85
  usage, care, 176–177
Work/availability, scope (discussion),
      109

Work, speaking up, 117
World, speaking up, 117

Y
Yelling, reaction, 179

Z
Zoom titles, 5–6